SOCIAL CRISIS
AND
SOCIAL DEMORALIZATION

The Dynamics of Status
in American Race Relations

RONALD A. KUYKENDALL

SOCIAL CRISIS AND SOCIAL DEMORALIZATION:
The Dynamics of Status in American Race Relations
Copyright © 2005 by Ronald A. Kuykendall

Arissa Media Group
P.O. Box 6058
Portland, OR 97228
Tel: (503) 972-1143
info@arissamediagroup.com
http://www.arissamediagroup.com

Printed and bound in the United States of America.

First Edition, 2005.

Library of Congress Control Number: 2005922437

International Standard Book Number: 0-9742884-3-8

Cover design by Matthew Haggett
Edited by Ariana Huemer

Arissa Media Group, LLC was formed in 2003 to assist in building a
revolutionary consciousness in the United States of America. For more
information, bulk requests, catalogue listings, submission guidelines, or
media inquiries please contact Arissa Media Group, LLC, P.O. Box 6058,
Portland, OR 97228. Tel: (503) 972-1143.
info@arissamediagroup.com • http://www.arissamediagroup.com

To the loving memory of my mother and father
Edith Viola Young Kuykendall and Harold Kuykendall, Sr.

To my wife
Janelle Moore Kuykendall

CONTENTS

Introduction

The issue of race relations, that is, racial antagonism, racial antipathy, and racial inequality is a persistent problem within the United States. The race problem is disturbing because of the contradictory and conflicting ethical, moral, and irrational predicaments produced by situations of race relations. Several divergent explanations have arisen for the problem of race relations. These explanations disproportionately focus on African Americans and the deviant or pathological aspects of that group. Considerable attention has been given to a particular subpopulation of the African American citizenry described as the "underclass": an unassimilated, socially and economically disadvantaged subculture with all the classic attributes of dysfunctionality. However, to speak of an underclass, although it may provide some objective reference to social position, is purely artificial and imaginary. The concept only makes sense to those conceiving of it. Such a class cannot be objectively differentiated, as it has neither members nor organization. What this term actually refers to is status: how others think of and treat individuals, as well as how those persons see themselves in the eyes of others. Consequently, behavior is towards persons and not towards class. Because the explanations are really attempts at explaining the dysfunctionality of individuals within the African American population, race becomes the significant variable.

The debate has frequently revolved around whether race relations are determined by race or by class with a racial bias. On the race side two different perspectives emerge: (1) the dysfunctionality within the African American population is an effect of inherent factors or traits that are deficient or abnormal; (2) the dysfunctionality within the African American population is an effect of racial antipathy, and hence prejudice and discrimination are the source of inequality and the resultant social and economic problems.

On the class side, the focus is on stratification within American society and within the African American population. The stratification is a consequence of economic factors that have dislocated or left behind a significant segment of the African American population, exacerbating dysfunctionality. The lack of socio-economic resources, rather than specific racial prejudice and discrimination, is the culprit that has caught this segment of the African American population unprepared to take advantage of economic changes.

The most widely held explanations about racial inequality and racial discrimination fall into three broad categories: deficiency theories, bias theories, and structural theories. This categorization is taken from the work of sociologist Mario Barrera (1979), and each will be considered here in turn.

Deficiency Theories

The contention of deficiency theories is that racial inequality and the concomitant social pathologies associated with African American behavior are located in either biological or cultural deficiencies. Therefore, the problem is an inherent inadequacy within African Americans.

Biological explanations, which assert that intellectual differences (read as intellectual deficiencies) are due to biological inheritance, have relied on IQ test scores. Although this category of explanation is held in scientific disrepute, it continues to stir considerable interest and even assert some degree influence (Gordon 1987; Hernstein 1971; Hernstein and Murray 1994; Jensen 1969, 1973; Wilson 1978).

Psychiatrist Frances Cress Welsing (1991) presents an inverse biological deficiency theory in which she asserts,

> [T]he quality of whiteness is indeed a genetic inadequacy or a relative genetic deficiency state, based upon the genetic inability to produce skin pigments of melanin (which is responsible for all skin color). The vast majority of the

world's people are not so afflicted, which suggests that color
is normal for human beings and color absence acts always as
a genetic recessive to the dominant genetic factor of color-
production. Color always "annihilates" (phenotypically and
genetically speaking) the non-color, white. Black people
possess the greatest color potential, with brown, red and
yellow peoples possessing lesser quantities respectively"
(4).

In Welsing's theory the psychological response of Europeans to their
color inferiority is a defensive and uncontrollable hostility and aggression
towards people of color. Combined with white demographic disadvantage,
whites' genetic inferiority leads to psychological defense mechanisms such
as <u>repression</u>, <u>reaction formation</u>, <u>projection</u>, and <u>displacement</u>. Thus,
racism and white supremacy are psychological responses, both conscious
and subconscious, to this sense of genetic inadequacy faced by whites.

Cultural explanations locate racial inequality and African
American social pathologies within abnormal or deviant cultural traits
such as weak family structure, language handicaps, lack of work discipline,
present rather than future orientations, dependency, and lack of success
orientation. They emphasize cultural deficiencies as being responsible for
the development of attitudes and values that limit opportunities or prevent
escape from poverty. This "tangle of pathology" sets in motion a vicious
circle resulting in drug addiction, crime, low educational achievement,
and economic problems that reinforces the weak family structure and
perpetuates abnormal and deviant cultural traits. Thus, it is not racism or
genetics but African American cultural adaptations that are responsible for
inequality and social pathologies (Auletta 1982; Banefield 1970; D'Souza
1995; Moynihan 1965; Murray 1984).

Bias Theories

Bias theories focus on prejudice and discrimination as the source
of inequality and the resultant social problems. Central to this analysis
is the idea that discrimination is due to racial prejudice. Thus, racism
stands out as the overriding factor responsible for not only inequality but
also psychosocial problems that inhibit and thwart social and economic
advancement (Bell 1992; Clark 1972; Grier and Cobb 1968; Hacker 1992;
Myrdal 1944; West 1994).

One such approach that fits within the bias theory model centers
on "symbolic racism." This approach makes the argument that racism
involves anti-black feelings combined with a perceived violation of

traditional American values. This dislike of African Americans is acquired through socialization and is expressed "in terms of abstract ideological symbols and symbolic behaviors of the feelings that blacks are violating cherished values and making illegitimate demands on the racial status quo" (McConahay and Hough 1976, 38). Additionally, images in popular culture represent majority-minority relations and can proscribe behavior, restrict change, and delimit collective action for change. These images--which can be subtle or obvious depictions of African Americans as subservient, subordinate, powerless, etcetera--while appealing to lower-echelon whites, "serves the interests of the upper class because it heightens identification of lower-class whites with their race instead of with their class" (Dubin 1987, 137).

Structural Theories

Structural theories postulate racial inequality and the consequent social problems of African Americans as a manifestation of economic relations. The source of African American inequality and social pathologies lies within the socio-economic structure of American society, that is, institutions and class structure.

One of the earliest such theories was the caste-class school, which asserted that the social structure, particularly within the American South, was a combined caste-class system in which whites of all classes occupy a dominant social position, and African Americans of all classes occupy a subordinate social position. Each person is born into, and lives within, his racially designated caste, with no opportunity for members to cross the caste line (Davis, Gardner and Gardner 1941; Dollard 1957).

Another structural approach popularized during the 1960s was "internal colonialism" or "domestic colonialism." This approach sought to describe a kind of colonialism in which dominant and subordinate racial groups exist within the same geographical location, but the subordinate racial group is subjected to systematic, structural discrimination within the economic realm, within the political system, and within the educational system in the interests of the dominant racial group. Racial ideologies emerge as justifications for relationships of domination, for the advancement of certain interests, and to fortify class positions (Allen 1969; Blauner 1972; Carmichael and Hamilton 1967; Cruse 1968).

Following the black power movement, domestic colonialism became "domestic neo-colonialism," in which America's corporate elite formulated a program to co-opt the black power movement and reduce its threat to economic and social stability, according to journalist Robert Allen (1969). Thus, asserts Allen, "blacks have been granted formal political

4

equality . . . [but] will continue to be a semi-colony of white America" (19-20).

The work of William J. Wilson (1978, 1987) also utilizes a structural approach and stands out as one of the more influential interpretations of this model. According to Wilson, changes in the American economy have dislocated, left behind, or altered the environment of a significant proportion of the African American population. And the social problems faced by this population must be understood in terms of economic organization. Structural economic changes in conjunction with historic discrimination, a deteriorating environment, government policies, and the disappearance of a viable African American middle class have subjected this segment of the African American population to a depletion of resources for economic stability.

Finally, there is in this area the Marxist conceptualization of racism as forming part of the superstructure and its ideological content. What emerges from this literature is that capitalist exploitation is responsible for the rise of racism (Alexander 1987; Cox [1948] 1970; Mason 1970; Schmitt 1988; Wallerstein 1974; Wolpe 1986).

Sociologist Oliver C. Cox ([1948] 1970) provides one of the most thorough and in-depth interpretations of race relations within a Marxian approach. For Cox, the concept of race relations and of race problems refers to the process of adjustment when "ethnics recognize each other physically and use their physical distinctions as a basis for the rationale of their interrelationships" (317). Hence, racial antagonism is "the phenomenon of the capitalist exploitation of peoples and its complementary social attitudes" (321). Thus, Cox hypothesizes that "racial exploitation and race prejudice developed among Europeans with the rise of capitalism and nationalism, and that because of the world-wide ramification of capitalism, all racial antagonisms can be traced to the policies and attitudes of the leading capitalist people, the white people of Europe and North America" (322).

As Cox sees it, racial exploitation is an attribute of the proletarianization of labor and a convenient device to maintain and preserve the exploitability of labor and resources; "[hence], racial antagonism is essentially political-class conflict" (333). Race relations are proletarian-bourgeois relations and therefore political-class relations. The only variation that race relations introduces to the phenomenon of class struggle is "the tendency of the bourgeois . . . to proletarianize a whole people--that is to say, the whole people is looked upon as a class--whereas white proletarianization involves only a section of the white people" (344).

Therefore, for Cox, the nexus between capitalism and race relations hinges on the fact that modern Western society is bourgeois capitalist--an exclusively European development that must, in order for capitalism to exist, proletarianize and consequently commodify labor. To commodify labor, "[the] capitalist is constrained to regard his labor power as an abstract quantity, a purchasable, <u>impersonal</u> commodity, an item in the cost of production rather than a great mass of human beings" (485). Thus, the immediate monetary interest of the bourgeoisie is to advance and promote an ideology and worldview that encourages and sustains proletarianization and, when necessary, uses force to effectuate this objective. And the development and exploitation of ethnocentrism is one aspect of this process that shows "by any irrational or logical means available that the working class of their own race or whole peoples of other races, whose labor they are bent upon exploiting, are something apart" (485-486). Hence, race prejudice is couched in rationalizations. As Cox explains,

> The intent of these rationalizations, of course, must always be to elicit a collective feeling of more or less ruthless antagonism against and contempt for the exploited race or class. . . . they must always have the intent and meaning that, since the race is inferior, superior people have a natural right to suppress and to exploit it . . . The rationalizations are thus a defense; race prejudice is a defensive attitude. The obtrusiveness of certain social ideals developed under capitalism as concessions to the masses makes the rationalizations of racial exploitation necessary (488).

Thus, Cox demonstrates the pivotal role played by economics in the formation of race relations and racial antagonism. As he interprets it, race relations are a manifestation of labor-capital-profit relations and hence are a part of class struggle.

An Alternative Explanation

Therefore, a different perspective is necessary to avoid the pitfalls of the previous theories and to synthesize, to some degree, the previous explanations. To accomplish this, the following explanation provides a historical insight into with the origin, evolution, and consequences of race relations within the U.S. between African Americans and European Americans. The following discussion will demonstrate that race relations are status relations from which can be deduced a series of behavioral consequences. I begin the discussion with the primary determinant in situations of race relations: social status. Social status determines where an individual begins his social existence; it also determines how an individual will live, where and in what condition he will live, how he will be reared, how he will be socialized, the extent of psychological suffering, and the magnitude of political repression. I next take up the first immediate consequence: social adversity. Prolonged and sustained social adversity is a lingering effect of the initial affliction of slavery. I then trace the effects of social adversity as they lead to a state of social crisis, a catastrophic situation involving internal conflict and a paroxysm of shifting emotions. Finally, I take up the result of social crisis: social demoralization. Social demoralization is a socio-psychological state that undermines confidence, discipline, willingness, and spirit. Afterward, I address the meaning of American nationhood within the context of race relations, as well as the political class nature of the race problem. I conclude with a discussion of political class struggle.

In the analysis that follows it should be kept in mind that the conceptual isolation of social status, social adversity, social crisis, and social demoralization are necessarily artificial and abstract. The occurrences of these socio-psychological states are not necessarily time bound; they are not individually specific to any historical period but recur throughout history and affect individuals idiosyncratically. And none of these factors, in and of themselves, cause human behavior, but rather interact interdependently and therefore provide clues and suggestions regarding race relations in the United States.

CHAPTER ONE

The Dynamics of Status in American Race Relations

In the following discussion I will identify four concepts through which American race relations might be understood. I will call attention to a particular way in which we can begin to think about race relations that diverges from some of the better-known notions of race relations. Specifically, I will call attention to social status as the primary basis for understanding race relations. Although 'status' is a legal term used to denote the standing of a person or group in relation to others, one of the vital determinants of individual behavior is an array of non-legal aspects. These may include all sorts of irrational values, sentiments, and beliefs and are the product of a dynamic process of interaction. The immediate effect of status is an emotional one, couched in the realm of covert feelings that may be referred to by such terms as "adversity," "crisis," and "demoralization." Explicitly, I assert that social status, once granted, determines the social existence of persons and groups, and this granting of status has both emotive and actual consequences culminating in real adversity, ultimately leading to feelings of crisis and demoralization. However, I must stress considerations of this kind are, at best, preliminary indications of a subject to be explored; they should be regarded as rough guidelines that may facilitate inquiry of a more empirical and historical kind. But whether this explanation serves to reveal the actual nature of race relations is a matter that can be resolved only by studying how status operates in particular social-historical circumstances.

Social Status

We can understand the race problem-- race relations, racial antagonism, racial antipathy, or racial inequality in the United States-- only if we recognize and understand the potent effects of social status: an individual's position in his society, which is a purely social phenomenon, a human contrivance based upon past and present human actions. The discipline of sociology has established the significance of social status and its necessity for maintaining social order, that is, social control. Status is socially granted and, in part, determines self-definition. The individual sees himself more or less as others see him and therefore behaves in a manner generally expected of one who occupies that particular status. The social granting of status comes about through situational factors, a process of interaction in which people's reactions to one another affect the responses of each. Although many factors determine social status, ascribed status is most important because it usually limits the character and number of achieved status positions for which an individual might be eligible. Once granted, ascribed status tends to be permanent, irrespective of the individual's own conduct. Therefore, to understand the effects of social status within the context of American race relations (and specifically regarding African Americans), we must start at the beginning.

The institution of slavery set the tone for race relations in the United States. Consequently, the psychosocial conditions of the initial status granted African Americans--that of slave--was socially reproduced or recreated and therefore made persistent. In order to maintain the status ascribed to African Americans, certain values and beliefs had to be collectively reproduced in the service of molding actions and attitudes that would ensure the ongoing subjugation of African Americans to the established social order.

Now, this does not mean that status is the only motive that enters into the shaping of human conduct. But it is a vital factor. Status determines where an individual begins his social existence. It also determines how, where, and under what conditions an individual will live; how he will be reared and socialized; and the extent of psychological suffering and political repression he will endure.

The earliest record of Africans' arrival in colonial America is dated 1619 at Jamestown, Virginia. Virginia was a political and economic leader in colonial America; it also, tragically, was "a leader in the gradual debasement of blacks through its ultimate institutionalization of slavery. It pioneered a legal process that assured blacks a uniquely degraded status--one in which the cruelties of slavery and pervasive racial injustice were guaranteed by its laws" (Higginbotham 1978, 19). Though originally not slaves but indentured servants (under a contractual arrangement in which a person served a master for a period of years), these Africans entered an existing social class system at the bottom of the social hierarchy. As pointed out by historian Carl N. Degler (1970), under an examination of the early history of slavery in the colonies "and the reaction of Englishmen

10

toward black men, it becomes evident that the assumption that slavery is responsible for the low social status of Negroes is open to question" (27). According to Degler, there is reason to believe that Africans in America were discriminated against well before the institution of slavery was codified. In Degler's opinion,

> [I]f one is seeking to uncover the roots of racial prejudice and discrimination against the Negro in America, the soundest procedure would be to abandon the idea that slavery was the causal factor. In place of it, one ought to work on the assumption that discrimination preceded slavery and by so doing helped to reinforce it. Under this assumption American race prejudice originated in the discriminatory social atmosphere of the early seventeenth century, long before slavery was written into law. When slavery did appear in the statutes, it could not help but be shaped by the folk bias within which it grew. Thus legal slavery in the English colonies reinforced and helped to perpetuate the discrimination against the black man that had prevailed from the beginning of settlement (28).

Degler justifies this assumption on the accounts of English attitudes toward black skin, or for that matter any non-white skin. The English consciousness of the African's differences were expressed in terms of the African's heathenism, which in literature was expressed with revilement and horror. This is seen, for example, in Othello and Titus Andronicus, where the African Moor is described as "sooty," "a thing," "spotted," "detested," "abominable," and "barbarous." Because "[N]egroes arrived in English America as the cargo of the international slave trade," this, according to Degler, "unquestionably fostered a sense of superiority among Englishmen" (29). Also, continues Degler, "the treatment accorded another dark-skinned heathen people, the Indians, offers further evidence that enslavement was early the lot reserved for Negroes" (29).

This observation was also made by political scientist Milton D. Morris (1992), who asserted that racism "goes beyond the purely black-white encounter in America and can be viewed as part of a larger 'disease' of cultural chauvinism which the colonists brought with them from Europe" (582). Historian George M. Fredrickson (2002) further places the association of blackness with slavery in the late Middle Ages, specifically within Iberia, where religion justified African slavery: "One possible rationale for holding Africans in servitude regardless of their religious status was the myth of the Curse of Ham or Canaan based on a mysterious passage in the book of Genesis" (43). This undoubtedly helped to inhibit condemnation of African slavery as contrary to Christianity and would later be used in the antebellum United States "to show that racial slavery was divinely sanctioned" (45).

This racialized religiosity made it easier for white European

11

Christians to dehumanize other human beings, particularly non-whites. As historian Don E. Fehrenbacher (1978) explains, "Whichever took root first in European thought, the association of Africans with slavery and the assumption of black inferiority had become firmly set and intertwined with each other before the first Negroes were landed in Virginia" (15).

Within several decades of arriving in Jamestown, the social and legal status of persons of African descent was determined on the basis of race. As pointed out by Judge A. Leon Higginbotham (1978), "Not all blacks in Virginia by the 1650s were slaves, but . . . the white colonists by that early date were already beginning to establish a process of debasement and cruelty reserved for blacks only" (26). Although slavery was not codified in Virginia law until 1661, by the 1640s "colonists began to give serious thought to the 'perpetual servitude' of blacks" (Franklin and Moss 1994, 56). Later, the Virginia slave codes so inferiorized persons of African descent "that their subhuman status deserved no recognition of human rights" (Higginbotham 1978, 39). The Virginia slave codes became a model for other colonies and firmly established the socio-economic status of persons of African descent. By 1705, Virginia's legislature "passed a comprehensive statute effectively removing blacks from the family of man and reassigning them to the classification of real property" (Higginbotham 1978, 50).

Thus, the social attitudes and policies of the white colonists defined not only the socio-economic status of Africans in America (and hence where they began their social existence), but also how they lived and in what condition they lived. Historian John W. Blassingame (1972) reports,

> The quantity, quality, and variety of food, clothing, housing, and medical care the slave received rarely satisfied him. The fact that another man determined how much and what kind of food, clothing, and shelter he needed to survive posed a serious problem for him. Equally serious was his dependence on the "average" amount of food and clothing his master decided was sufficient for all slaves (158).

With regard to housing, Blassingame points out that most slaves

> lived in crudely built one-room log cabins with dirt floors and too many cracks in them to permit much comfort during the winter months . . . Not only were the slave cabins uncomfortable, they were often crowded. Most of the cabins contained at least two families . . . Usually the slaves had to make what furniture and utensils they used. They built tables, beds, and benches and sometimes carved wooden spoons. Generally the cabins contained beds made of straw covered boards, and tables of packing boxes. Some slaves slept on the ground or on mattresses of corn shucks without

blankets (159-160).

Historians John Hope Franklin and Alfred A. Moss, Jr. (1994) also report,

> Housing for slaves was especially poor. The small, rude huts
> were usuallyinadequate as well as uncomfortable. Windows
> and floors were almost unheard of. Frederick Olmsted
> was shocked when he viewed the slave cabins on some
> plantations he visited. They were small and dilapidated with
> no windows, unchinked walls, and practically no furnishings
> . . . Many cabins were wholly without beds, and slaves were
> compelled to sleep on quilts or blankets with only some
> straw or shucks between them and the earth. The inadequacy
> of space was, if possible, even worse than the absence of
> comforts and conveniences. One Mississippi planter had
> twenty-four huts, each measuring sixteen by fourteen feet,
> for his 150 slaves (131).

Life on the plantation was generally barren, and recreation and
other diversions were extremely limited. "For slaves there was little in the
way of enjoyment and satisfaction during moments or hours they were off
the job" (Franklin and Moss, 1994, 133). The slaves' time was not their
own, and what little time the slaves could call their own was needed for
rest. As explained by Franklin and Moss (1994),

> Even if there was no work and even if an opportunity for
> diversion presented itself, slaves could never escape the
> fact that they were slaves and that their movements as well
> as their other activities were almost always under the most
> careful surveillance. If they found it possible to enjoy the
> periods when they were not on the job, they either possessed
> a remarkable capacity for accommodation or were totally
> ignorant of the depth of their degraded position (133).

Therefore, the physical existence of the African slave was wholly
determined by the slave-master.

Understandably, under such conditions child rearing was
neglectful. As former slave and abolitionist Frederick Douglass explained,
"The domestic hearth, with its holy lessons and precious endearments, is
abolished in the case of a slave mother and her children" (Blassingame
1972, 94). Booker T. Washington, another former slave who became a race
leader and educator experienced a similar fate and wrote, "My mother . .
. had little time to give to the training of her children during the day. She
snatched a few moments for our care in the early morning before her work
began, and at night after the day's work was done" (Blassingame 1972,
94). Additionally, slave children suffered from the violence of slavery.
Being forced to witness floggings and personal abuse of parents and loved

ones was undoubtedly a terrifying and painful lesson for the slave child. At the same time, slave parents were compelled to severely admonish their children as a way of "avoiding pain, suffering, and death" (Blassingame 1972, 99).

Given the physical hardship of slavery, obviously child bonding was difficult and child-rearing haphazard, since parental responsibility was consumed by work. Inferentially, child-rearing practices among slaves and the social institution of slavery profoundly affected the child's sense of self, his later object-relationships (that is, the child's social relational experience on psychological growth and personality formation), and his introduction to reality. When slave children reached their useful age (which was extremely early), child's play ended and "they settled down to the existence that was the inevitable lot of a slave" (Franklin and Moss, 1994, 133-134). Slave parenting by necessity required that slave children be reared to be slaves. As such, they were denied the normalcy of a childhood.

Consequently, the ascribed social status of Africans in America determined more than their class position within the social status gradient and their ensuing level of life and child rearing practices. It also determined the direction of socialization and effectively molded the African to fit the status. Slave children learned early what slavery was and how to survive in bondage. Some of the more important lessons were to hold their tongues around whites, not to rebel against their masters, to passively accept personal abuse and punishment of themselves and others, and to be obedient to the slave system. The powerful effects of slavery, in part, conditioned what slaves thought of themselves and significantly structured their personality. Lacking any civilizing inducements, slavery bred and encouraged indecency and cultural degradation among slaves. The slaves' very self-concept was a function of slave status.

As well as their position as property, their substandard living conditions, and the neglectful child rearing, slaves were also subjected to the constant watchful eyes of whites. They were exposed to every capricious, vengeful, or sadistic whim of their masters as part of the socialization process, including, for example, mutilation, flogging, and verbal abuse. For the slave women and girls there was the additional evil of forced cohabitation, licentious intercourse, and pregnancy. This experience is expressed by Harriet Jacobs, a young slave girl, who recounts,

> But I now entered on my fifteenth year—a sad epoch in the life of a slave girl. My master began to whisper foul words in my ear. Young as I was, I could not remain ignorant of their import. I tried to treat them with indifference or contempt . . . He was a crafty man, and resorted to many means to accomplish his purposes . . . He peopled my young mind with unclean images, such as only a vile monster could think of. I was compelled to live under the same roof with him--

where I saw a man forty years my senior daily violating the most sacred commandments of nature. He told me I was his property; that I must be subject to his will in all things. My soul revolted against the mean tyranny. But where could I turn for protection? . . . there is no shadow of law to protect her from insult, from violence, or even death; all these are inflicted by friends who bear the shape of men (Franklin and Moss, 1994, 138).

Thus, slave status provided the social and psychological matrix of the power relationship between the races. As explained by sociologist Oliver C. Cox ([1948] 1970), "The slavery situation is probably the purest form of established race relations "(357). As chattel, the slave was reduced to the same production and economic value as a beast of burden. Consequently, the exploitative basis of race relations under slavery reduced the bondsman to a sub-social level upon which the master class contrived, ideologically, their exploitative interests. The essential part of this ideology was the inferiority of the slave. Hence, the slave was denied rights, social and geographical mobility, and any social communication that contradicted or quarreled with the master. As an instrument of production, the slave was "completely below the level of conscious organization and direction of community life" (357). Psychiatrists Abram Kardiner and Lionel Ovesey (1951) make a similar observation:

The relation of a man to a slave is quite the same as to a horse, and yet there are important differences. It is the same, insofar as the prime objective is to exploit the utility value of the slave, and to perpetuate the conditions which favor his maximum utility. All other conditions for cultural existence are ignored or prevented by force . . . In order to carry out the program of maximum utility of the slave, it was necessary to suppress all cultural practices which were injurious to utility and permit only those over which no control could be exercised (42-43).

In addition to its physical punishment, slavery also imposed a psychological punishment. As a sign of disapproval and a very important technique of social control, this was another key element in the socialization process. Slavery's traumatic psychological punishment engendered atypical personality consequences that secured conformity. Psychiatrist Kardiner and Ovesey (1951) assert,

The psychological effects of the slave status on the individual were probably very complex; but a few features of this adaptation can be inferred with certainty: (1) Degradation of self-esteem. (2) Destruction of cultural forms and forced adoption of foreign cultural traits. (3) Destruction of the family unit, with particular disparagement of the male. (4) Relative enhancement of the female status, thus making her the central figure in the culture, by virtue of her value to the male for sexual ends and as mammy to the white children. (5) The destruction of social cohesion among Negroes by the inability to have their own culture. (6) The idealization of the white master, but with this ideal was incorporated an object which was at once revered and hated. These become incompatible constituents of Negro personality (47).

Connected to the psychological punishment of slavery is the place of "honor" in any social order. Those who lack honor or are prohibited from competing for it are really outside the social order; in a word, they are "dishonored." According to sociologist Orlando Patterson (1982), such was the position of the slaves, whose dishonor "sprang . . . from that raw, human sense of debasement inherent in having no being except as an expression of another's being" (78). Consequently, the success and effectiveness of the slave system required, in Patterson's words, "that the slave population nurse its sense of dishonor, accept its dishonored condition, or find alternative means of expressing or sublimating its grievances" (97). However, Patterson points out,

> There is absolutely no evidence from the long and dismal annals of slavery to suggest that any group of slaves ever internalized the conception of degradation held by their masters. To be dishonored—and to sense, however acutely, such dishonor—is not to lose the quintessential human urge to participate and to want a place. Indeed, it is precisely this irrepressible yearning for dignity and recognition that is hardest to understand about the condition of slavery. The fundamental problem posed by slavery may be simply stated as one of incentive and mutual recognition (97).

The very fact that dignity was monstrously denied the slave made the slave ever more passionately desirous of it. Subsequently, the slave was, according to Patterson, "afire with the knowledge of and the need for dignity and honor," and thus, "assertions that the slave internalized the degraded conceptions of him held by the master; or that his person was necessarily degraded by his degraded condition" (100) are very superficial.

To say that no slave ever internalized the degradation perpetrated by his or her white masters is too unequivocal. Any established social system, according to psychiatrist Frances Cress Welsing (1991), will assign social roles to those born into the system "inasmuch as children are born to parents who already are occupying 'their place' in the structured social system" (240). And one's position in the social system, continues Welsing, partly determines identity, and "one's identity" in an oppressive social system "is either that of the oppressor or that of the oppressed" (240).

As an inferiorized people, the oppressed are subjected to very stressful and negative social and environmental experiences. Consequently, continues Welsing, "negative and stressful experience, which is structured to affect every aspect of life activity, leads to the development of self-and-group-destructive behavioral patterns" (242).

According to historian John W. Blassingame (1972), oppression was so great that many slaves were thoroughly convinced about "their master's claim about rightness, the power, and the sanctity of whiteness and the degradation, the powerlessness, and the shame of blackness" (199). Some passionately wished they were white, as indicated by ex-slave James Watkins, who declared, "I felt as though I had been unfortunate in being born black, and wished that I could by any means change my skin into a white one, feeling certain that I should then be free" (199).

This desire for whiteness was still present in the twentieth century, as revealed by sociologist E. Franklin Frazier (1962) in an interview with a seventeen-year-old African American youth:

> However, knowing that there are difficulties that confront us all as Negroes, if I could be born again and had my choice I'd really want to be a white boy . . . I wouldn't care to be lighter or darker and be a Negro . . . I realize of course that there are places I can't go despite my family or money just because I happen to be a Negro. With my present education, family background, and so forth, if I was only white I could go places in life. A white face holds supreme over a black one despite its economic and social status. Frankly, it leaves me bewildered (177-78)

Of further note on this subject, psychiatrist Ronald Laing (1967) observes:

> All those people who seek to control the behavior of large numbers of other people work on the <u>experiences</u> of those other people. Once people can be induced to experience a situation in a similar way, they can be expected to behave in similar ways. Induce people all to want the same thing, hate the same thing, feel the same threat, then their behavior is already captive . . .(95).

In such a relationship, the oppressed embody the projected degradation of their oppressors and thus collude with their oppressors and compliment the oppressors' identity. That is, both oppressor and oppressed engage in a counterfeit act of mutual self-deception based on pretense, finding in one another confirmation of the false self that each is attempting to make real. In the process, both become estranged from themselves and hence become guilty of self-betrayal. This collusion maintains the illusions and delusions that impede each person's capacity to discover his true self. Having been ascribed a particular position, "attributions 'put him in his place' and thus have in effect the force of injunctions" (Laing 1969, 132). Whatever others attribute to someone, either implicitly or explicitly, plays a decisive part in forming that person's "sense of his own agency, perceptions, motives, intentions: his identity" (Laing 1969, 132). Consequently, an authentic sense of self is undermined.

Lastly, Brazilian educator Paulo Freire (1970, chap. 1) writes perceptively about the effects of oppression. He explains that oppression, whether individual or collective, is any situation in which one individual exploits or hinders another individual's pursuit of self-affirmation. Thus, oppression is an actual, specific situation that shapes and conditions the structure of thought displayed by the oppressed, and this shaping and conditioning manifests itself in several forms. The situation of oppression produces an adhesion to, and identification with, the oppressor. The oppressed absorb the oppressors within themselves. This impairs the perceptions of the oppressed about themselves and their situation. At this point, the oppressed do not see themselves as the antithesis of the oppressors, but rather see the oppressor as a model. This partly explains why the oppressed occasionally become oppressors or sub-oppressors of their friends, associates, and companions; why the oppressed display self-destructive behavior like addictions, suicide-homicide, abuse of family members, and crime; and why the oppressed are attracted toward the oppressor's way of life striving to resemble, imitate, and follow the oppressor. In this way, the oppressor lives within the oppressed. As hosts of the oppressor, the oppressed cannot perceive that without them, the oppressor could not exist. Oppression subjugates the oppressed, making them into beings-for-another. This adhesion to the oppressor creates within the oppressed a fear of freedom. It generates a fear of autonomy and responsibility that would come with ejecting the oppressor. This fear inhibits the oppressed and is expressed in feelings of inefficiency, powerlessness, emotional dependence, risk aversion, and greater oppression. Ultimately this culminates in self-depreciation, worry, doubt, suspicion, and fatalism.

Therefore, as asserted by Laing (1969), "To understand the 'position' from which a person lives, it is necessary to know the original sense of his place in the world he grew up with. His own sense of his place will have been developed partly in terms of what place he will have been given in the first instance by the nexus of original others" (117). Consequently, a person's experience of his position is structured and curtailed by the influence of others. Others contribute all the time to a person's existential position, and this structuring and curtailing is often internalized by that person, becoming an integral part of his attitudes and beliefs and inevitably affecting behavior.

The low status of African Americans has been additionally sustained through political repression. Governmental policy historically has reflected social practice; therefore, norms and mores of race relations were enforced through the law. By the time of American independence, the problem of slavery was being reevaluated. Even Thomas Jefferson addressed the issue in the Declaration of Independence, laying at the door of King George III the responsibility and perpetuation of slavery as a violation of human nature "in the persons of a distant people who never offended him, captivating and carrying them into slavery in another hemisphere, or to incur miserable death in their transportation thither" (Franklin and Moss 1994, 71). However, the allusions to slavery "were unacceptable to the Southern delegation at the Continental Congress and were stricken from the document" (Franklin and Moss 1994, 71). Although some slaves were freed as a condition of serving in the war, slavery remained a way of life for the overwhelming majority of the African population.

As an independent nation, America entertained the issue of slavery in the debate over western expansion. The Ordinance of 1784, which was a plan to cede land to the Confederation for future states, was amended by just a single vote to delete provisions abolishing slavery after 1800. Thomas Jefferson noted that this single vote "would have prevented this abominable crime from spreading itself across the country" (Fehrenbacher 1978, 77).

The adoption of the federal Constitution ensured the continuation of slavery. Although slavery was declining in the Middle Atlantic and New England states, it remained very much alive in the Southern states. For example, James Madison, as a condition of Southern support for the federal Constitution, justified the controversial compromise of counting slaves as three-fifths of the population. In doing so, he asserted,

> [T]hat representation relates more immediately to persons, and taxation more immediately to property, and we join in the application of this distinction to the case of our slaves. But we must deny the fact that slaves are considered merely as property, and in no respect whatever as persons. The true state of the case is that they partake of both qualities: being considered by our laws, in some respects, as persons, and in other respects as property. In being compelled to labor, not for himself, but for a master; and being subject at all times to be restrained in his liberty and chastised in his body, by the capricious will of another--the slave may appear to be degraded from the human rank, and classed with those irrational animals which fall under the legal denomination of property. In being protected, on the other hand, in his life and limbs, against the violence of all others, even the master of his labor and his liberty; and in being punishable himself for all violence committed against others--the slave is no less evidently regarded by law as a member of the society, and not as part of the irrational creation; as a moral person, not as a mere article of property. The federal Constitution, therefore, decides with great propriety on the case of our slaves, when it views them in the mixed character of persons and property.

This is in fact their true character (Federalist No. 54).

Even though the federal Constitution neither subscribed to nor expressly forbade the abolition of slavery (in fact, the word is not even mentioned in the document), it acknowledged the existence and continuance of the institution. The issue of slavery through "various influences and circumstances conspired not only to involve the United States government with slavery but to make it in some degree a sponsor and protector of the institution" (Fehrenbacher 1978, 37). This involvement with slavery was no doubt enhanced by the very location of the nation's Capitol in Washington D.C., a slave-holding community with its own slave code put into effect by federal authority. It was further enhanced by slave-owning presidents, cabinet members, and congressmen who assisted in the normalization and legitimation of slavery.

Time and again, the issue of slavery and its expansion would permeate government business. Beginning with the Fugitive Slave Law of 1793, slavery and the status of persons of African descent would remain a constant fixture in national politics. The issue of slavery played a prominent role in the Louisiana Purchase, the Missouri Compromise, the congressional "gag rule" of 1836 (which tabled all antislavery petitions), the annexation of Texas, the Mexican American War, the Compromise of 1850, the Kansas-Nebraska Act, the Dred Scott case, and, ultimately, the Civil War.

Following the Civil War and the constitutional abolition of slavery, the federal government by legal action during Reconstruction attempted to guarantee to former slaves the rights of citizenship, first through the Civil Rights Act of 1866 and later through the Fourteenth and Fifteenth Amendments to the Constitution. In 1875, Congress enacted even more thorough legislation in another Civil Rights Act that guaranteed African Americans the right to jury duty as well as equal rights in all public accommodations and means of transportation. However, "emancipation" had freed African American labor, "but without the possibility of equal participation in the culture of which he was now proclaimed a part. Mobility was nominally his, but actually, not at all. He had no more opportunity for participation than he had before, and in addition, he had now to compete for opportunities to work, at a great disadvantage. His status was actually unchanged . . ." (Kardiner and Ovesey 1951, 48). When the Compromise of 1877 made Rutherford B. Hayes president, the federal government made few attempts to enforce civil rights on behalf of African Americans, and as historian Rayford W. Logan ([1954] 1965) points out, "the entire South had regained the right to resume its plans for social engineering . . . During the next quarter of the century, the South sought to have the Constitution interpreted, federal laws repealed or rendered innocuous, and Northern public opinion made amenable to the end that Negroes should become what were later called second-class citizens" (22).

Consequently, American race relations took on a bipartite situation, that is, a society dichotomized into color groups. As pointed out by historians John Hope Franklin and Alfred A. Moss, Jr. (1994), whites made the decision to completely separate the races. By 1870, southern states began enacting laws that prohibited racial intermarriage and separated the races on trains, in depots, and on wharves. By the 1880s, African Americans were banned from white hotels, barbershops, restaurants, and theaters; southern states required separate schools; and in 1896, the Supreme Court constitutionally recognized segregation in its "separate but equal" doctrine set forth in Plessy v. Ferguson (262). The bipartite situation became the norm, secured by segregation barriers and rationalizations. In such a situation, being white is a cultural advantage; cultural degradation of African Americans is a must.

Following the civil rights movement of the 1960s, de jure segregation was eliminated and since then, some African Americans have significantly improved their social and economic positions. As well, African Americans have made substantial gains particularly in the areas of politics and education. The number of African Americans elected to public office has increased. The proportion of African Americans completing high school is nearly equal to that of whites, and the proportion of African Americans attending and completing college has increased. But widespread de facto segregation and racial prejudice remains a problem.

Therefore, can it be argued today that African Americans are still plagued by racist social attitudes and polices that define their socio-economic status and hence, where they begin their social existence? Can it be argued today that current, racist social attitudes and policies determine how African Americans live, including child-rearing practices? Can it be argued today that racist social attitudes and policies impact the direction of African American socialization? Can it be argued today that African Americans suffer psychological problems as a consequence of racist social attitudes and policies? And, can it be argued today that African Americans today experience political repression?

Poverty, joblessness, teenage pregnancy, female-headed families, welfare dependency, and crime disproportionately plague African Americans, particularly within the inner cities. Today, a significant proportion of African Americans begin their social existence in poverty. Consequently, African Americans remain underrepresented in high-status professional, technical, and managerial positions, while they are over-represented in service occupations, traditionally recognized as low-status jobs. Therefore, African American individual and family income is substantially lower than that of average Americans, and the net worth of African American households is significantly lower.

Also, a significant proportion of African Americans begin their social existence in segregated neighborhoods with low to moderate-income housing. These neighborhoods tend to be infested with substandard housing, squalor, noise, unemployment, crime, deterioration, and neglected children.

Racist social attitudes and policies are partly to blame for this kind of social existence. Regardless of anti-discrimination legislation and white perceptions that minorities receive preferential treatment in hiring, the reality proves otherwise. Several studies have demonstrated that African American job applicants with identical qualifications of white applicants are three to five times less likely to receive the job offer. Furthermore, white applicants are more likely to advance further in the hiring process and are less likely to receive rude, unfavorable, or discouraging treatment (Turner, Fix, and Struyk 1991).

Residential racial discrimination is no different. Despite federal legislation outlawing discrimination in the sale or rental of housing, some in the housing industry continue to discourage African Americans from buying or renting homes and apartments in white neighborhoods. There is also considerable white, organized neighborhood resistance to proposals for low-income and moderate-income housing. Studies have also shown that African American applicants for home loans are rejected more often than white applicants. Even applications of high-income African Americans are rejected more often than those of low-income whites (Massey and Denton 1987, 1988). So, racial discrimination still defines the socio-economic status of African Americans and where they begin their social existence.

The above discussion is significant for understanding how racist social attitudes and policies determine how African Americans live and in what conditions they live. Employment discrimination and residential discrimination affects the African American standard of living and overall quality of life. Such pressures affect child rearing and socialization because of the unique frustrations and difficulties that accompany a low plane of living. African American parents today, just as those living during times of slavery, must socialize their children to live in and deal with a society where racial prejudice and discrimination are aimed at them. Thus, the parent-child relationship and the socialization process are significantly affected by the objective socio-cultural conditions that penetrate the home.

Attitudinal discrimination, which is often overt and visible, remains prevalent. Racial prejudice permeates every aspect of African American life and continues a demeaning reality to which African Americans are consistently exposed. Attitudinal discrimination is seen, for example, when whites move out of neighborhoods when African Americans move in. It is seen when African Americans receive poor service in restaurants, stores, hotels, or business services. It is seen in police brutality, police harassment, and racial profiling of African Americans by law enforcement officials. African Americans of every social class and profession are vulnerable targets for racial prejudice and discrimination. Such incidents are constant sources of tension and anticipation, as described by one African American professor, who states,

> [B]eing black in America is that you have to spend so much time thinking about stuff that white people just don't even have to think about. I worry when I get pulled over by a cop. I worry because the person that I live with is a black male,

and I have a teen-aged son. I worry what some white cop is going to think when he walks over to our car, because he's holding on to a gun. And I'm very aware of how many black folks accidentally get shot by cops. I worry when I walk into a store, that someone's going to think I'm there shoplifting. And I have to worry about that because I'm not free to ignore it. And so, that thing that's supposed to be guaranteed to all Americans, the freedom to just be yourself is a fallacious idea. And I get resentful that I have to think about things that a whole lot of people, even my very close white friends whose politics are similar to mine, simply don't have to worry about (Feagin 1991, 114).

Another African American, Judge Bruce Wright (1993) describes how even financial success is no shield to deeply-ingrained racist attitudes:

One afternoon, during a trial, I felt so faint and weak I could not carry on. The clerks, with affectionate concern, feared that I was having a heart attack. I was taken out of the courthouse lashed to a stretcher . . .

In the emergency room of the hospital, I was placed in a curtained-off area where there were two beds some distances apart. On one was a white man, obviously one of the poor derelicts now and then brought in from the Bowery. He appeared to be in a state of joyous alcoholic bewilderment. He needed a shave; neither his soiled sneakers nor his socks matched; he drooled a bit and sang softly in garbled syllables.

As I watched him from my bed, I felt pangs of pity. He seemed much worst off than I. I felt guilty for being dressed in a three-piece suit and clean shirt.

I heard a nurse outside the curtain area say, "Hurry, doctor, we have a judge who is ill." A white doctor parted the curtains, paused at the entrance, looked at me and then at the white derelict. He hurried to the side of the white man, lifted his wrist, as though to test his pulse, and said, "Judge, what seems to be the matter?"

It was a bracing experience, wholly therapeutic, and I began to recover without delay.

The most remarkable aspect of the hospital experience was the reinforcement of my view that whites almost automatically have a "place" reaction to the color of dark skin. Compared with a poor, ragged, homeless white unfortunate, unshaven and drooling, a well-dressed black simply could not be the judge (24-25).

And even when the discrimination is subtle and less readily visible the result is the same. Although institutionalized discrimination appears to be impersonal, it reinforces the overall racist social attitudes and its consequences. Racist social attitudes have placed African Americans at a disadvantage. Therefore, economic changes play a significant role in sustaining African American inequality and lower socio-economic status. Consequently, the lingering effect of a degraded socio-economic status in slavery persists. Once granted, social status endures regardless of the individual's conduct or achieved status. Being black in the United States is persona non grata, as is clearly demonstrated in this parable, presented by political scientist Andrew Hacker (1992) to his white students:

> You will be visited tonight by an official you have never met. He begins by telling you that he is extremely embarrassed. The organization he represents has made a mistake, something that hardly ever happens.
>
> According to their records, he goes on, you were to have been born black: to another set of parents, far from where you were raised.
>
> However, the rules being what they are, this error must be rectified, and as soon as possible. So at midnight tonight, you will become black. And this will mean not simply a darker skin, but the bodily and facial features associated with African ancestry. However, inside you will be the person you always were. Your knowledge and ideas will remain intact. But outwardly you will not be recognizable to anyone you now know.
>
> Your visitor emphasizes that being born to the wrong parents was in no way your fault. Consequently, his organization is prepared to offer you some reasonable recompense. Would you, he asks, care to name a sum of money you might consider appropriate? He adds that his group is by no means poor. It can be quite generous when the circumstances warrant, as they seem to in your case. He finishes by saying that their records show you are scheduled to live another fifty years--as a black man or woman in America.
>
> How much financial recompense would you request (31-32)?

Most white students respond by asking for $50 million, a calculation that "conveys, as well as anything, the value that white people place on their own skins" (32). Obviously this large sum of money buys protections, or at least softens the calamity of discrimination and hazards they expect to face as African Americans. This is clearly an acknowledgement of the low status of African Americans and the significance of race in America.

Finally, African American political repression is indicative of the way African Americans are made invisible and ignored by the political system. African American public opinion tends to be obscured by the opinion-shaping apparatus (that is, mainstream institutions, agencies, and the media) that leaves the determination of truth and reality to the (non-African American) majority population. African American political participation is restricted by closed or semi-closed political organizations, at-large systems in local elections, and redistricting plans that dilute and fragment African American voting strength. Even when African American voter participation is substantial in determining the outcome of an election, it does not translate into jobs, services, and sympathetic treatment. The professionalization of local and state politics, the decline of political machines, the entrenchment of civil-service employees, and the encroachment by the federal government on state and local government power have all limited the opportunities for African American political and economic advancement. In fact, the federal system provides numerous devices for the legal, constitutional, and administrative defeat of significant egalitarian change. Hence, a significant proportion of African Americans are today systematically locked into a lower status position.

What can be concluded from the foregoing information is that the institution of slavery set the tone for race relations in the United States; it was here that African Americans were given a status beneath the bottom of the white social hierarchy. This status established not only the socio-economic position of Africans in America, but also how they lived, where and in what condition they lived, how they were reared, how they were socialized, and the power relationship between the races. And although this status has been reevaluated from time to time, it has never been resolved, not even by a new government. Although the system changed from slavery to a bipartite situation to the elimination of legal segregation, the consequences of a degraded, dehumanizing, and psychologically-punishing social status lingers on today. The African American's position within the United States system of stratification has grossly affected his life chances. On every dimension of social stratification--class, status, and power--African Americans have occupied a subordinate position. Lacking honor and prestige, the African American's status today is intimately related to his past class position of slavery. Consequently, African Americans as a whole today wield little or no power. Racism was established as an ideology to make this social inequality acceptable. Religion was used to support slavery and segregation; science has been used to justify a racial hierarchy; and meritocracy has been used as proof that African Americans lack intelligence, industriousness, motivation, and ambition to take advantage of opportunities. Consequently, the effects of the African American's place in the system of stratification have influenced his life expectancy, cause of death, mental and physical health, and lifestyle. As observed by psychiatrists William H. Grier and Price M. Cobbs (1968),

> We must conclude that much of the pathology we see in black people had its genesis in slavery. The culture that was born in that experience of bondage has been passed from generation

to generation. Constricting adaptations developed during some long-ago time continue as contemporary character traits. That they are so little altered attests to the fixity of the black-white relationship, which has seen little change since the birth of this country (24-25).

Social Adversity

Understandably, the lowly slave status granted Africans in America became an obstacle to achieving other status positions and consequently thwarted, reduced, or otherwise prevented the requisite social satisfactions necessary for normal individual human growth, development, and well being. Since slavery made skin color a condition of status, the person of color was socially and economically restricted. Whether enslaved or free, the person of color was legally and/or socially prevented from achieving other status positions-- for example, occupationally, educationally, materially, residentially.

The kind and severity of social adversity is directly related to one's social status. A slave faces many obstacles and frustrations of a quality and quantity unimaginable by the non-slave. In the racially-segregated society, the subordinate race encounters barriers and restrictions that are reserved for them alone; even when racial discrimination is legally prohibited the racially-stereotyped, stigmatized out-group is still confronted with barriers and restrictions--although at times of a more or less subtle and sophisticated nature--that have the same adverse effects as legal discrimination and segregation. Hence, adversity was a precondition of enslavement, fostered through punishment, pain, and myth. It affected the psychosocial functioning of African Americans, leaving them susceptible to division, degradation, and deviance. This social adversity was further compounded by political adversity. Thus, the initial status of slave engendered a prolonged and sustained condition of social adversity.

The very act of enslavement is an adversity. The slave-master imposes his or her objectives on the slave, taking possession of him or her. The act reduces the slave to the status of a non-sentient thing. As a thing, the slave has no rights and is therefore subject to the will of the slave-master. Consequently, as asserted by philosopher G. W. F. Hegel, the slave-master "has as his substantive end the right of putting his will into any and every thing and thereby making it his, because it has no such end in itself and derives its destiny and soul from his will" (Knox [1952] 1981, 41). This power over a thing constitutes possession, and as property or a thing the slave is not free, not a person, and without rights. The slave and master "exist as two opposed shapes of consciousness; one is independent consciousness whose essential nature is to be itself, the other is the dependent consciousness whose essential nature is simply to live or be for another" (Knox [1952] 1981, 115).

As pointed out by philologist and philosopher Friedrich Nietzsche, the master class is self-serving, intolerant, and must prevent anything that is contrary or impending to its values. This type "feels <u>himself</u> to be the determiner of values, he does not need to be approved of, he judges, 'what harms me is harmful in itself,' he knows himself to be that which in general first accords honor to things, he <u>creates values</u>" (DeLue 1997, 292). In contrast to the master class, there is the slave point of view, "abused, oppressed, suffering, unfree . . . uncertain of themselves" (DeLue 1997, 293). Oppressed by the master class, the slave distrusts the values of the master class, sees little in it that is good, necessary, or of interest to the slave. However, to the master class, the slave's point of view and way of life is seen as that of "good-natured' and '<u>harmless</u>' people, who are 'easy to deceive, perhaps a bit stupid" (DeLue 1997, 294). But slaves do not always willingly accept their subordinate position. Such a position is adverse, breed's resentment and hatred, and fuels a drive for resistance.

Another aspect of enslavement, and hence adversity, is that it is conditioned through severe punishment and excruciating pain. As previously mentioned, as part of the socialization process African slaves were subjected to physical punishment. The experience teaches slaves to repress their natural drives and instincts. It is a cruelty that molds the slave to uphold the rules and customs; it is a cruelty that burns forever into the slaves' collective memory. As recorded in <u>The Interesting Narrative of the Life of Olaudah Equiano, or Gustavus Vassa, the African</u> (1972), he recalls that he "was often a witness to cruelties of every kind, which were exercised on my unhappy fellow slaves" and included "violent depredations on the chastity of the female slaves," hanging, burning, cutting, mangling, and shackling (26). Moses Roper, in <u>A Narrative of the Adventures and Escape of Moses Roper, from American Slavery</u> (1972), recalls how tar was poured over his head and face and set on fire. On another occasion his fingers were put in a vice and his nails squeezed off. And on yet another occasion his feet were put on an anvil and beaten until some of the nails came off (216). According to historian John W. Blassingame (1972), slaves were routinely flogged, kicked, slapped, cuffed, or had their ears boxed; they were frequently "branded, stabbed, tarred and feathered, burned, shackled, tortured, maimed, crippled, mutilated, and castrated" (p. 163-64).

In its contemporary form, conformity to domination is no longer inflicted through physical pain, but as Nietzsche says, "by forging within the consciousness of individuals a sense of guilt for contemplating or for engaging in actions that violate the norms of society" (DeLue 1997, 300). But when forced to suppress what is natural and instinctual, the mind ends up at war with itself; it becomes a mind turned backward against itself. Full of emotions such as "cruelty, joy in persecuting, in attacking, in change, in destruction . . . these emotions have as their target those who hold them, and thus they are 'turned against the possessors of such instincts'" (DeLue 1997, 300-301). The individual develops toward his or her own-self hostile emotions. Nietzsche described this as "bad conscience," a serious illness that necessarily creates for people a sense that they are prisoners within their own minds, without hope of achieving freedom. It is no wonder, then, that in a society that generates bad conscience each person is a 'desperate prisoner,' 'rubbing himself raw against the bar of his cage.' It is understandable as well that for such individuals, their willfulness is completely vanquished (DeLue 1997, 301).

French historian Michel Foucault expanded Nietzsche's conception in different terms. Using Jeremy Bentham's model prison, the Panopticon, to address this issue, Foucault demonstrated how the individual internalizes social control or how power is exercised over the individual's life without physical force. It is a scenario in which the prisoners are under the constant gaze of the guards and become so overly conscious of the guards' gaze that, in effect, the guards become part of the prisoners' imagination, even when the guards are not present. Unable to escape the guards' presence, the prisoners therefore act and behave accordingly, as if voluntarily, without force. It is a form of subtle coercion, which "exercises power over people as it is internalized and made a part of each person's consciousness" (DeLue 1997, 306). Foucault described the development of this experience as a "technique of human dressage by location, confinement, surveillance, the perpetual supervision of behavior and task, in short, a whole technique of management, which the prison was merely one manifestation" (DeLue 1997, 306). In this way, social control is transposed from its external existence into an internal existence; opposition to the status quo is thus reduced or destroyed.

To sustain the status quo, whether in slavery, in the bipartite situation, or in contemporary society, the disposition of myths is indispensable as justifications. Consequently these myths, including those that state that African Americans are naturally inferior; that they are lazy, dishonest, and criminal; and that they are uneducable, engender more adversity. These myths, which are essential to African Americans' continued subjugation, are not only believed and asserted by whites, but also internalized by African Americans themselves. They serve the purpose of legitimizing the status quo through various strategies, identified by sociologist John B. Thompson (1990, 60-66) as legitimation, dissimulation, unification, fragmentation, and reification. These strategies construct and convey meaning in the social world and hence in domination. They establish domination by law; concealment and denial; standardization; differentiation and expurgation; and naturalization, nominalization, and passivization.

According to Thompson, legitimation can be expressed through typical strategies of rationalization, universalization, and narrativization. Rationalization involves a self-satisfying but incorrect process of reasoning that defends or justifies a complex of social relations or institutions. Rationalization persuades others that it is worthy of support through, for example, biological theories of racial inequality. Universalization represents social relations and institutional arrangements as serving everyone's interests and as being open to all when, in fact, such relations and institutions are closed and serve the interests of only some. An example of universalization might be the assertion that meritocracy is the basis of success, regardless of race. Narrativization refers to treating the present as part of a past tradition through stories, speeches, documentaries, histories, novels, films, and jokes. One such example is the southern representations and celebrations of the confederacy.

Dissimulation entails concealing, denying, obscuring, or deflecting attention from existing relations and processes. Strategies of dissimulation include displacement, euphemization, and trope. Displacement, a psychological defense mechanism, involves shifting the reference of feelings, impulses, objects, or individuals to another target, thereby transferring the positive or negative connotations. This strategy has often been used against African Americans by scapegoating them for a multiplicity of social ills. Euphemization is the substitution or description of social relations or institutions in such a way as to elicit positive valuations-- for example describing the violent suppression of legitimate protests as maintaining "law and order." Trope is the figurative use of language (such as synecdoche, metonymy, and metaphor) as a method of misrepresentation-- that is, describing something as though it is something else. Examples of trope include racial stereotyping and the use of symbols to imply, without explicitly stating, a negative association. An example might be equating welfare or criminality with African Americans by showing a black face when discussing or demonstrating these issues.

Unification subsumes individuals into a collective identity without consideration of the differences and divisions separating them. This mode typically takes the form of standardization and symbolization of unity. Standardization is the adoption of criteria promoted as commonly shared and accepted such as racism, which serves to create a collective identity among whites and to legitimize hierarchy among racial and ethnic groups. Symbolization of unity is the construction of symbols such as flags, emblems, or inscriptions that serve to unify and reaffirm a collective identity. Southern celebrations and representations of the confederate flag is one such example of symbolization.

Fragmentation involves splintering those individuals and groups who challenge or threaten the status quo. Strategies of fragmentation include differentiation and expurgation of the other. Differentiation means calling attention to distinctions, differences, and divisions that disunite individuals and groups-- effectively thwarting any challenges to the existing social relations. This includes, for example, the constitutional legitimation of the "separate but equal" doctrine that legalized "Jim Crow," as well as the use of race as a wedge issue to dissuade political cooperation between African Americans and working-class whites. Expurgation entails demonizing another in order to manufacture an enemy that individuals as a collective are called upon to resist or extirpate. Examples of the demonization of African Americans are abundant throughout American culture, such as the implied predatory, criminal intent of African American males.

Finally, reification treats transitory, impermanent events as natural. This mode takes the forms of naturalization, eternalization, and nominalization (also known as passivization). Naturalization involves taking a socially-constructed event, such as racism, and treating it as inevitable and natural. Eternalization, like naturalization, involves taking a socially-constructed event like racism and depriving it of historicity as though it were permanent, unchanging, and recurring, thus embedding it in social life through repetition. Nominalization and passivization refocus attention on certain themes at the expense of others through transforming actions into nouns, by deleting actors and agency, and rendering verbs into the passive form, thus omitting a subject. For example, it may be said that "the policy is under consideration" or that "satisfactory solutions for discrimination are being sought" instead of identifying a specific subject or an actor.

In these ways, myths become an element of social fantasy, an internalized set of relations and operations designed to work on the experience of the participants in the social relationship. Each participant internalizes the fantasy, that is, myths that convey the experience of being part of the social relationship. Thus, the myths, or the social fantasy, give meaning in the service of power; they structure the relations of domination.

Such an experience has grossly affected African American psychosocial functioning and easily explains what psychiatrists William H. Grier and Price M. Cobbs (1968) describe as "cultural paranoia" among African Americans, "a high degree of suspicion toward the motives of every white [person]" (135). The racial experience and environment of the African American demands such a paranoid posture. According to Grier and Cobb, it is necessary for the African American to distrust whites and to

> be on guard to protect himself against physical hurt. He must cushion himself against cheating, slander, humiliation, and outright mistreatment by the official representatives of society. If he does not so protect himself, he will live a life of such pain and shock as to find life itself unbearable. For his own survival, then, he must develop a cultural paranoia in which every white [person] is a potential enemy unless proved otherwise and every social system is set against him unless he personally finds out differently (149).

Cultural paranoia is thus a symptom of the pathological American social, political, and economic structures and manifests itself in African American psychology. The American social, political, and economic structures are pathological in the sense that they have produced dehumanizing and psychologically destructive social behaviors among its citizens. This kind of behavior is not inherent in the human condition or circumstantial of the complexity of society. Rather it is the particular form of social organization that has become part of the social heritage. Thus, we are born heirs to this pathological condition and continue its propagation without being conscious of its fundamental motivation. Because cultural paranoia is a response by African Americans to their condition and treatment in America, it is a reaction to racism. Thus, cultural paranoia is a by-product of racial antagonism that is structured by social, economic, and political factors.

Another way of looking at this experience is what novelist Richard Wright ([1957] 1964) described as "acting," a life situation that "evokes in them [African Americans] an almost unconscious tendency to hide their deepest reactions from those who they fear would penalize them if they suspected what they really felt" (17). African American poet Paul Laurence Dunbar taps into this experience in his poem "We Wear the Mask":

> We wear the mask that grins and lies,
> It hides our cheeks and shades our eyes,--
> This debt we pay to human guile;
> With torn and bleeding hearts we smile,
> And mouth with myriad subtleties.
>
> Why should the world be overwise,
> In counting all our tears and sighs?
> Nay, let them only see us, while
> We wear the mask.
>
> We smile, but O great Christ, our cries
> To thee from tortured souls arise.
> We sing, but oh the clay is vile
> Beneath our feet, and long the mile;
> But let the world dream otherwise,
> We wear the mask!

Historian Carter G. Woodson ([1933] 1990) also expresses this experience when he asserts,

> [T]he Negro's mind has been brought under the control of his oppressor. The problem of holding the Negro down, therefore, is easily solved. When you control a man's thinking you do not have to worry about his actions. You do not have to tell him not to stand here or go yonder. He will find his "proper place" and will stay in it. You do not need to send him to the back door. He will go without being told. In fact, if there is no back door, he will cut one for his special benefit. His education makes it necessary.
> The same educational process which inspires and stimulates the oppressor with the thought that he is everything and has accomplished everything worth while, depresses and

crushes at the same time the spark of genius in the Negro by making him feel that his race does not amount to much and never will measure up to the standards of other peoples. The Negro thus educated is a hopeless liability of the race (xiii).

After literally centuries of such treatment, African Americans transmitted their suspicion and caution toward whites through subcultural socialization. As a means of maintaining "social clarity and humanistic insight," cultural paranoia became a "collective fusion and culmination of black intellectual and experiential substance" (McClendon 1983, 20). Thus, cultural paranoia is a defense mechanism that has sustained African American survival. It is not a result of chance, nor is it a psychological invention; it is the result of logical connections that take place objectively and independently of the individual and deduces itself.

Another adverse consequence of African American lower status is the susceptibility to division. Division is facilitated through whites' interference in African American organizational efforts, favoring certain representatives or leaders of the African American community, softening up those who reveal leadership potential, and selectively distributing benefits and penalties. Such divisive actions exploit "the weak points of the oppressed: their basic insecurity . . . Under these circumstances, the oppressors easily obtain positive results from divisive action" (Freire 1970, 141). Historian John W. Blassingame (1972) points out that during slavery it was not unusual for masters to compel some slaves to help control the others and then reward them or point to them as models for emulation. Black slave drivers were used to maintain plantation rules and given the authority to punish other slaves. Domestic servants acted as secret police and as extensions of the master's eyes and ears. Often flattered and materially rewarded, trained to speak glowingly of their good treatment before visitors, "the domestic servant was a valuable adjunct to the slaveholder's security and public relations staff" (161).

Political scientist Frances Fox Piven and sociologist Richard A. Cloward, in their classic work Poor People's Movements (1977), demonstrate the modern divisive and placating efforts of political elites to maintain the status quo. First concessions are offered "to remedy some of the immediate grievances, both symbolic and tangible, of the disruptive group" (29). Second, cooptation is exercised, "by making efforts to channel the energies and angers of the protestors into more legitimate and less disruptive forms of political behavior, in part by offering incentives to movement leaders" (30). Third, support for the protesting group is undermined by creating "new programs that appear to meet the moral demands of the movement, and thus rob it of support without actually yielding much by way of tangible gains" (30-31). Finally, repression is employed against those "leaders and groups who are more disruptive, or who spurn the concessions offered [by singling them] out for arbitrary police action or for more formal legal harassment through congressional investigations or through the courts" (31). The numerous examples of these strategies include eliminating de jure segregation, offering movement leaders jobs or appointments within the status quo bureaucracy, the Great Society programs and affirmative action, and the Counterintelligence Program (Cointelpro) of the Federal Bureau of Investigation.

An additional aspect of adversity is described by Brazilian educator Paulo Freire (1970) as cultural invasion, wherein the oppressors "penetrate the cultural context of another group, in disrespect of the latter's potentialities; they impose their own view of the world upon those they invade and inhibit the creativity of the invaded by curbing their expression" (150). Hence, those invaded are objects molded and acted upon by the invaders; they incorporate the oppressor's way of thinking into their own thinking; their reality becomes that of the oppressor and not their own. They "become convinced of their intrinsic inferiority [and] alienated from the spirit of their own culture and from themselves" (151).

But as pointed out by sociologist Oliver C. Cox ([1948] 1970), "The cry that the Negroes are inferior is an illusion; what is real is the fierce insistence by the white ruling class that Negroes do nothing which might lead either themselves or other people to believe that they are equal or superior to whites" (366-367). This state of degradation serves to prove that African Americans are undeserving of social equality, and, as Cox continues, the white ruling class seeks "through myriad and powerful devices, to make the colored person, as a human being, ashamed of his very existence; indeed, the accomplishment of racial shame is a psychological goal . . ." (367). This is also observed by sociologist Gunnar Myrdal (1944), who writes,

> The low plane of living . . . and all the resulting bodily, intellectual, and moral disabilities and distortions of the average Negro make it natural for the ordinary white man not only to see the Negro is inferior but also to believe honestly that the Negro's inferiority is inborn. This means . . . that all attempts to improve the Negro by education, health reforms, or merely giving him his rights as a worker and a citizen must seem to be less promising of success than otherwise would be. The Negro is judged to be fundamentally incorrigible and he is, therefore, kept in a slum existence which, in its turn, leaves the impact upon his body, and soul which makes it natural for the white man to believe in his inferiority (101).

This situation amounts to imprisonment, and "this imprisonment provides the proper milieu for the planned cultural retardation of the colored people. Here they may mill and fester in social degeneracy with relatively minimal opportunity for even the most ambitious of them to extricate themselves" (Cox [1948] 1970, 382). Forced to accommodate himself to discrimination and color prejudice, the African American, says Cox, is very much in "the situation of a very ugly person or one suffering from a loathsome disease who is made to feel suspected or exposed. The suffering which this is likely to engender may be aggravated by a consciousness of incurability and even blameworthiness, a self-reproaching which tends to leave the individual still more aware of his loneliness and unwantedness" (383). Understandably, such a situation has a devastating effect upon the personality. Once again, Cox notes that the "socio-psychological pressure of color prejudice" destroys "the individual's self-respect," making him feel ashamed and socially inconsequential (383). Isolated, excluded, and alienated, the African American more or less internalizes and accepts the prejudiced system's racial conception.

The stigmatization endured by African Americans can be more easily understood as an example of sociologist Erving Goffman's (1963) insightful analysis of stigma, which he explains can be either: (1) discredited stigma, which is readily visible (such as physical deformity); or (2) discreditable stigma, which is not immediately obvious. For the most part, African Americans' membership in a racial group that is often viewed negatively by whites puts them in the position of a discredited stigma, wherein they have come to expect hostile responses in their social interaction with whites. On the other hand, the African American who is physically indistinguishable from his white counterparts is in the position of a discreditable stigma and therefore is confronted with a whole set of different problems. Such persons may decide to "pass" if their appearance does not betray them and consequently participate in the social advantages accorded whiteness and assume full membership in the white race. However, others might "shuttle," that is, move back and forth between the two races and consequently face greater risk of detection because concealment becomes cumbersome (Cox [1948] 1970, 430).

Now, if a person has been ascribed a subordinate, inferior status maintained by violence and brutality, obviously such a person would look, feel, and behave in a socially deficient manner. The ascribed status dictates, more or less, clearly defined and specific signs of recognition. In other words, the ascribed status, in part, determines the appearance and behavior of its members. It is not at all unusual to ascertain the status of others almost entirely based on how they look and behave. As indicated earlier, the individual's self-conception is a function of status. So, the individual not only looks and behaves according to the status; he feels the status. A person who is deprived socially, culturally, economically, politically, and emotionally will both appear deviant and behave in a deviant manner. The African slave was subordinated and inferiorized in order to make him look like a slave, feel like a slave, and behave like a slave. Slavery, by definition, assumes the slave is deficient, flawed, impaired, weak, and inferior. Consequently, the African slave was not privy to social and cultural inducements of formal education, family stability, career choice, and economic opportunity. He was denied the simplest personal courtesies such as a warm welcome, friendly attention, or being listened to or talked to with some degree of respect. Even among free blacks during the antebellum period, freedom was nominal. Restrictive laws and attitudes ensured the maintenance of a slave-like status. In many places they were required to carry a certificate of freedom, were subjected to surveillance and curfews, were restricted in their movement, were denied the right to vote or serve on juries, were discriminated against in employment, and were segregated in public places (jails, hospitals, parks, burial grounds, theaters, hotels, restaurants, transportation systems, etc.). This kind of treatment was not just endemic in the South but was practiced in the New England states, the Old Northwest, and Western states (Meier and Rudwick 1970).

Social adversity is intimately related to a group's state of mind regarding its future. Some may be unwilling to endure such social difficulties and are provoked to change the status quo (however random or irrelevant the attempt), while others are willing to tolerate considerable social difficulties. But, as historians John Hope Franklin and Alfred A. Moss, Jr. (1994) note, "It cannot be denied that as old as the institution of slavery was, human beings had not . . . brought themselves to the point where they could be subjected to it without protest and resistance" (140). Hence, slaves reacted in various ways to the adversity and brutality of slavery: escape through ritual and song, loafing on the job, feigning illness, sabotage, self-mutilation, suicide, homicide, running away, and revolt. Following Reconstruction and the establishment of the bipartite system, African Americans addressed social adversity through self-help associations (Frazier 1964; Thomas 1991; Yearwood 1980). Other organizations such as the National Association for the Advancement of Colored People, the National Urban League, the Universal Negro Improvement Association, the Nation of Islam, the Southern Christian Leadership Conference, and the Black Panther Party for Self-Defense (just to mention a few) responded to social adversity through protests, demonstrations, boycotts, appeals to the courts, appeals to Congress and the president, and cultural nationalism and separation.

In general, the African American approach to social adversity has primarily been expressed in either assimilationist/integrationist tendencies (that is, the struggle for racial equality) or separatist/nationalist tendencies (i.e., the struggle for complete autonomy and self-determination), or both. These two strands of thought have often contended for ascendancy, as pointed out by historian Sterling Stuckey (1987):

> The cyclical pattern that saw integrationism and nationalism vying for ascendancy owes much . . . to a misreading or neglect of the past--a problem endemic to integationist leaders in black America from 1830 onward. The period from 1830 to 1860, in which the forces of integrationism and nationalism first seriously contended for ascendancy, prefigured similar struggles among black Americans in the twentieth century. Those early years were years in which integrationists--spiritually rootless leaders with little sense of the relationship between people's liberation and the historical process--were countered by

nationalists, who marked out the material and to some extent the spiritual lines along which genuine liberation might be attained (231).

According to sociologist Oliver C. Cox ([1948] 1970), the African American approach to the race problem and social adversity is primarily directed at satisfying the "urge among Negroes to assimilate" (545) by overcoming the opposition among whites. In fact, asserts Cox, the drive toward assimilation is so compelling that African American group solidarity is forfeited in favor of unrestricted participation in white enterprises and institutions, and were it not for racial discrimination, African American enterprises and social institutions would not exist (546). Hence, African Americans continually address themselves toward eroding away such limitations that prevent their recognition as qualified Americans. Cox additionally asserts that the advance in social status of a subordinate group requires a concession by the dominant group; however, such a concession would require an admission by the dominant group that the subordinate group rightfully deserves such inclusion. This is precisely what African Americans strive to achieve (569).

Achieved status, like ascribed status, is socially granted but with one significant difference: Ascribed status, which is given at birth, is, for African Americans, nearly permanent, no matter how they might strive to escape the stigma. This ascribed, racial status limits what other status positions can be achieved by limiting the character, quality, and number of achieved status positions for which one is eligible. Furthermore, although achieved status is predicated on personal accomplishment, it is a social reward granted by whites and it is subject to withdrawal. Like ascribed status, it is a potent force for social control. Consequently, even those African Americans who have achieved status positions, from physicians to professors to congresspersons, are never quite secure in these achieved status positions. They are always aware of how difficult it was to reach that position from an inferior ascribed status and how the achievement is always qualified by a racial designation. On this point sociologist E. Franklin Frazier (1962) observes

> Both men and women among the black bourgeoisie have a feeling of insecurity because of their constant fear of the loss of status. Since they have no status in the larger American society, the intense struggle for status among middle-class Negroes is . . . an attempt to compensate for the contempt and low esteem of the whites. Great value is, therefore, placed upon all kinds of status symbols . . .
> There is much frustration among the black bourgeoisie despite their privileged position within the segregated Negro world. Their "wealth" and "social" position cannot erase the fact that they are generally segregated and rejected by the white world (180-81).

This racial designation somehow seems to denigrate the accomplishment and reduces the quality of the achievement. Consequently, the African American is forever at a distinct disadvantage, and while it is possible for any African American to achieve status, his chances to do so are considerably less compared to whites of any social class. The costs are higher and the motivations, aptitudes, and mannerisms conducive to success are less often acquired out of an ascribed, lower-status, African American background.

Having undergone the traumatic experience of slavery, the African American was emancipated without any preparation, provision, or qualification for equal participation. Displaced and reestablished in a new status position through political cataclysm, African Americans were understandably uncertain of themselves, suspicious of the motives of whites, and unable to believe with assurance that their new status was real. This mistrust proved not unfounded, as African Americans went from being emancipated slaves to second-class citizens--another subordinate, inferior status replete with the social, cultural, economic, and political disadvantages of slavery.

Reconstruction would do little to alleviate this. As pointed out by historian August Meier and sociologist Elliot Rudwick (1970), "Almost any attempt of Negroes to realize their hope for a racially egalitarian society could call forth violent repression from whites" (173). Between 1866 and 1872, African Americans were victimized by riots in throughout the South. By 1877 even the so-called white friends of African Americans had deserted them. As pointed out by Meier and Rudwick, "All in all, the Northern whites--including many former abolitionists--found it relatively easy to pay the price of sectional reconciliation. The price was the rejection of the idea of a racially egalitarian society--and even the desertion of the black's fundamental constitutional rights" (176). This violent reaction to racial equality can partly be explained by white fear, which placed stringent rules and isolation on the African slave and non-slave populations. As pointed out by political scientist Milton D. Morris (1992), "white Americans had always been fearful of the seething black slave population and the prospect that it might one day rise up and destroy its oppressor" (588). This fear, according to Morris,

> has been a strong force in shaping white attitudes toward blacks, and in influencing the style and content of white politics. Even now it constitutes one of the principal bases of white hostility to black efforts at changing their lot in society. It played a large part in the development of one-party politics in the South and was almost the only issue in Southern politics for generations. Its impact is equally pervasive outside the South, as indicated by the pattern of responses to the varied expressions of black discontent during the 1960s . . . Only an overpowering or what Holden terms

"pathological" fear explains such bizarre twists in American politics as the enormous popularity achieved by George Wallace as a candidate for President in 1972 . . . capitalizing on white fears by resurrecting racism as a "respectable" theme in American national politics. These contemporary manifestations of fear by whites make it easy to grasp the nineteenth-century passion to suppress and control the black population (589).

But this fear is also associated with guilt. The guilt referred to here is not necessarily indicative of a sense of personal responsibility, but rather of defensiveness. This point was made by political scientist Andrew Hacker (1992) who asserts that

white Americans, regardless of their political persuasions, are well aware of how black people have suffered due to inequities imposed upon them by white America. . . . Yet white people who disavow responsibility deny an everyday reality: that to be black is to be consigned to the margins of American life. It is because of this that no white American, including those who insist that opportunities exist for persons of every race, would change places with even the most successful black American. All white Americans realize that their skin comprises an inestimable asset (60).

Consequently, according to Hacker, whites may vehemently oppose programs that seem to benefit African Americans, because it is a way of denying "to themselves that the value imputed to being white has injured people who are black" (60). This also explains, according to Hacker, "why white people devised the word 'nigger' and gave it so charged a meaning" (61). To them, it justified slavery and rationalizes segregation and subordination. But it also is a way whites can avoid confronting the "nigger" in himself or herself. The "nigger" thus becomes a necessity that shields the "nigger" within whites. Since only blacks can be niggers, "it follows that none of its [niggerness] attributes will be found in white people" (61).

Finally, by the time de jure segregation eliminated the legally-sanctioned, second-class status of African Americans, their long-standing subordination had left the marks of oppression: poverty, joblessness, low educational achievement, weak family structure, and all the other social problems that come with social disorganization and subjugation. As reported by the Joint Center for Political and Economic Studies (2000), the proportion of African American children living with a single parent doubled from 22% in 1960 to 55% in 1998. Correspondingly, the proportion of African American children living with two parents declined, falling from 60% in 1970 to 35% in 1998.

Racial differentials in poverty also remain enormous. In 2001,

22.7% of African Americans lived at the poverty level, compared to 7.8% of whites. Among African American children under 18, the poverty rate was 30.2% compared to 9.5% for white children, and the poverty rate for African Americans 65 and over was 21.9% compared to 8.1% for whites (see Table 1). Concurrently, African American income lags behind that of whites. Nearly half of married white couples earn $75,000 and over, compared to only ¼ of married African American couples. Also, over half of single African American women earn less than $25,000 (see Table 2).

African Americans continue to lag behind whites in education, even though the proportion of African Americans completing high school and college has steadily increased (see Table 3). But regardless of their educational attainment, African Americans across the board earn less than whites, which translates into the fact that African American educational achievement is worth less than white American educational achievement (see Table 4).

African Americans are also disproportionately represented in prisons. According to Human Rights Watch (2000), "In every state, the proportion of blacks in prison exceeds, sometimes by a considerable amount, their proportion in the general population." Not surprisingly, this phenomenon can be traced back to emancipation, when a steady increase in African American incarceration began. According to historians Mary Frances Berry and John W. Blassingame (1982),

> [I]n the state of Georgia, there were only 183 prisoners confined in the penitentiary in1858, all of whom were white. In 1870 there were 393 persons confined, of whom 59 were white and 334 were black. According to the U.S. census, the total number of blacks confined in southern federal and state prisons in 1870 was 6,031; ten years later the number had increased to 12,973; twenty years later there were 14,244; and in 1904 there were 18,550. The commitment rate for blacks in 1904 was higher than that for whites . . . However, for certain immigrants, the rate was higher than for blacks . . . The commitment rate for immigrants declined as they became absorbed into American life. But blacks remained unassimilated and with a higher commitment rate (232).

Additionally, legal changes do not necessarily result in attitudinal changes. De facto segregation and discrimination remain as real problems. As reported by the Lewis Mumford Center (2002, 2001), segregation still exists in education and in neighborhoods, which works to the benefit of whites. According to the Center, white students are "in very different schools from minority students, and particularly in schools with less class disadvantage," and "whites live in neighborhoods with low minority representation while minorities live in neighborhoods with high minority representation." So although there have been some social, educational, economic, and political improvements, African Americans are still perceived, in general, as lower status persons who are incapable, unqualified, undeserving, or otherwise suspect. The perception, which is manifest in the social environment and is recognized by some African Americans, maintains for them a sense of doubt, caution, mistrust, and hesitancy that makes them stand out in adverse contrast to white Americans.

From day one, the African entered the socio-economic structure within colonial America at the very bottom of the social hierarchy. Unlike Africans who immigrated to old Europe, Africans did not arrive in America seeking the benefits of an expanding economy and opportunities for economic advancement. Instead, they were dropped off a Dutch ship as "twenty Negars" (Degler 1970, 26). African slaves quickly displaced indentured servants and thus began the "causal connection between the institution of slavery and the color prejudice of Americans," which would leave a deep and enduring impression upon the character and future of African Americans (Degler 1970, 27). It was "the pattern of slavery as conditioned by past and present history and ecology, and manifested in particular forms of class rule, [that] determined race relations" (Genovese 1969, 4). The disabilities of slavery would so inferiorize the African American that the maladjustments associated with it would appear deceptively natural. Subjected to violence and contained by brutality,

> the slave was natally alienated and condemned as a socially dead person, his existence having no legitimacy whatever. The slave's natal alienation and genealogical isolation made him or her the ideal human tool . . . perfectly flexible, unattached, and deracinated. To all members of the community the slave existed only through the parasite holder, who was called master . . . the slave holder fed on the slave to gain the very direct satisfactions of power over another, honor enhancement, and authority. The slave, losing in the process all claim to autonomous power, was degraded and reduced to a state of liminality (Patterson 1982, 337).

Hence, as psychiatrists Abram Kardiner and Lionel Ovesey (1951) point out,

> Once you degrade someone in that way, the sense of guilt makes it imperative to degrade the object further to justify the entire procedure. If you do not use the human being whose attributes you despise, you can escape the ambit of his influence by pure avoidance; if you use him, you cannot avoid the consequences. The only defense now is to hate the object . . . Now the reasons for the hatred becomes the loss of dominance over an object that has already been degraded in status. This represents a claim by the Negro for a reciprocal emotional relation with the white and hence a fall in status

for the white (379).

Thus, racism, whether overt or surreptitious, is the struggle to salvage white status by keeping African Americans in their place. Cultural assimilation in this situation is incompatible with exploitation, because "assimilation diminishes the exploitative possibilities" (Cox [1948] 1970, 336). The persistent handicaps, pathologies, and difficulties experienced by a significant segment of the African American population today are a consequence of slavery. Slavery (and later the bipartite system) necessarily curtailed and perverted the existence of the African American masses. Largely unassimilated, racially ostracized, culturally repressed, and socially isolated, contemporary African American existence is a product and achievement of white racism. The social adversity faced by African Americans reflects their status position in the class structure--restricted opportunities, social dislocations, and social isolation are symptomatic of racial-class inequality.

Social Crisis

As noted by sociologist Richard T. LaPiere (1954), " . . . progressive adversity leads people to doubt and then abandon their hope for the future--i.e., the ultimate fulfillment of their social expectations--and thus lose their faith in the inherent value of the traditional social practices, devices, and structures by which those expectations are normally fulfilled . . ." (534).

As this occurs, the social situation is redefined as a social crisis. A social crisis, like an individual crisis, is "a functionally debilitating mental state resulting from the individual's reaction to some event perceived to be so dangerous that it leaves him or her feeling helpless and unable to cope effectively by usual methods" (Dixon 1979, 10). It is a critical situation in which hostile internal forces reach a turning point and are in the most tensed state of opposition; the social situation is no longer tolerable or manageable, and a decisive change is impending. The parties involved are overwhelmed by emotions and unable to reason effectively. And although each person's capacity for stress and pressure is idiosyncratic, "everyone has a breaking point at which habitual patterns of adaptation and problem-solving methods are no longer effective in maintaining the usual degree of social functioning" (Dixon 1979, 11). Just as in a catastrophe, the person(s) become stressed and may go into psychological shock. In this condition, although the body internally is mobilized for action, the individual cannot act because his previous patterns of behavior have been interrupted. However, at some point the pressure becomes intolerable, and the person acts randomly and irrelevantly; this person is in a panic.

Consequently, a social crisis, like and individual crisis, is a subjective state; it is the personal meaning attributed to some event that reduces cognitive functioning, which includes information processing,

41

thinking ability, perception, memory, planning, and problem-solving methods. This emotional state is precipitated by some event or events giving rise to anxiety, feelings of helplessness, diminished defenses, and emotional disequilibrium. As a result of the excessive emotionality, the person in either individual or social crisis experiences personality disorganization that may be "characterized by habitual acting out or impulsive, irresponsible, or antisocial behavior" (Dixon 1979, 10).

This is what happens when social crisis evolves from prolonged and sustained social adversity, as is the case with African American society. As pointed out by LaPiere (1954),

> An individual who has come gradually and as the result of repeated and intensifying adverse experiences to doubt the inherent value of a traditional device or procedure has undergone a significant and relatively durable personality change. He has acquired new values, sentiments, and interests and possibly new motivations; and these new personality attributes have been superimposed upon those attributes which previously led him to accept and utilize the traditional device or procedure . . . Since the acquisition of the new attributes does not wipe out the old, with which they are in opposition, the individual experiences internal conflict (535-536).

As long as the internal conflict does not grow, intensify, or become acute it can be endured. However, LaPiere (1954) continues,

> [W]hen internal conflict is both intense and increasing, as it is likely to become under conditions of progressive social adversity, the individual may finally reach a point at which the stress is intolerable and, like an overstrained piece of metal, break psychologically. That point is . . . a psychological crisis; he may either restructure his personality in such a way that one or another of the conflicting sets of personality attributes is more or less rejected or else rejecting both sets, he may invent a new set of attributes, i.e., become psychopathic (536).

Thus, the social adversities discussed in the previous section emerged from African Americans' lowly status and induced a state of social crisis. African Americans have reacted to their social crisis in the identifiable ways of any person in crisis: by divorcing themselves from the perceived cause (in this case white racial antagonism) through isolation, avoidance, escapism, or pathological behavior. It is a mental state similar to what Nietzsche described as "bad conscience"-- self-destructive, hostile emotions turned against the self. Psychiatrist Frantz Fanon (1968) described this as "the period when the niggers beat each other up" (52).

It is aggressiveness turned backward against the self, and what Fanon called "collective autodestruction" (52) and "one of the ways in which the [oppressed] muscular tension is set free" (54). It is, Fanon says, where "we discover the kernel of hatred of self which is characteristic of racial conflicts in segregated societies" (304). Psychiatrist Alvin Poussaint (2000) described this situation as "posttraumatic slavery syndrome," that is, the persistent presence of racism within a culture of oppression has created a physiological risk for African Americans that have "taken a tremendous toll on the minds and bodies of black people" (15).

Two African American novels--Native Son by Richard Wright and Beloved by Toni Morrison--poignantly recreate the effects of social crisis induced by adversity, lowly status, and racial oppression. Wright creates in Native Son's protagonist, Bigger Thomas, a painful and undeniably real portrait of an African American male deformed by the American racial system into a double murderer. But it is not the murder of Bessie, an African American woman, that disrupts the social universe and causes ripples. Rather, it is the murder of Mary Dalton, a white woman, which brings all forces of society against Bigger. Mary Dalton's murder is spurred by Bigger's experience of race relations in America. He knows that for an African American male to be caught in the bedroom of a drunken white woman, no matter how innocent the situation, is catastrophic. Bigger's resultant fear and panic precipitates a crisis. In an attempt to silence Mary's drunken verbalizations that might alert others to his presence, Bigger accidentally suffocates her, which intensifies the crisis. From this point forward, Bigger's experience parallels that of the rodent in the opening chapter. The rat leaves the safety of his hole and is immediately confronted with danger. Having moved beyond the boundaries established by Bigger's family, the rat has disrupted the tranquility of the family's universe and thus must be hunted down and destroyed. So too is the fate of Bigger, who leaves Chicago's South Side and enters into an alien white environment; he too disrupts the tranquility of the universe and as a result must be destroyed.

Toni Morrison creates a similar portrait of an African American female deformed by the American racial system. Sethe, the main character in Beloved, too is a murder-- but of her own child. What would provoke a mother to do such a thing? As Morrison makes clear, so traumatized by the experience of slavery was Sethe that she perceived murder as her only recourse to being returned to this condition. When slave catchers come to return Sethe and her children into slavery, Sethe is so panicked by this prospect that she commences to kill her children. The thought of returning to slavery is so intolerable and emotionally overwhelming that Sethe breaks psychologically. Her only option, given her debilitating mental state, is murder.

This situation of social crisis is eloquently portrayed in the classic work of African American psychiatrists William H. Grier and Price M. Cobbs, Black Rage (1968). In this work, the authors reveal the devastating psychosocial affects of slavery, discrimination, and racism on African

Americans; they demonstrate with clarity and therapeutic skill that the African American's "inner suffering is due largely to a hostile white majority" (2). The shadow of the past has filled African Americans with grief, sorrow, bitterness, and hatred; eventually the emotional conflict reaches a flash point, the rage cannot be swallowed, and a crisis is at hand. As pointed out by Grier and Cobbs, "People bear all they can and, if required, bear even more. But if they are black in present-day America they have been asked to shoulder too much. They have had all they can stand. They will be harried no more. Turning from their tormentors, they are filled with rage" (1-2). As slaves, African Americans were stripped of everything and physically abused. Even after slavery ended, the abuse continued in thoughts, feelings, intimidation, and even in lynching. Consequently, as Grier and Cobbs assert, "The culture of slavery was never undone for either master or slave. The civilization that tolerated slavery dropped its slaveholding cloak but the inner feelings remained. The 'peculiar institution' continues to exert its evil influence over the nation. The practice of slavery stopped over a hundred years ago, but the minds of our citizens have never been freed" (20).

The evidence of crisis-induced, internal conflict is present in the historical record. The initial act of enslavement was traumatic and shocking. Some of the captives went insane, gave up the will to live, or committed suicide (Blassingame 1972, 7). According to historians John Hope Franklin and Alfred A. Moss, Jr. (1994), "Self-mutilation and suicide were popular forms of resistance to slavery" (142). Slaves rendered themselves ineffective as workers by cutting off their toes and hands. Suicide was prevalent, and slave mothers murdered infants to prevent them from growing up as slaves.

Having endured the catastrophe of slavery, Africans were emancipated at the end of the Civil War. The expectation was their freedom would be permanent and their social interaction with whites would be more harmonious. As citizens, they expected the privileges that citizenship offered. But whites had quite different ideas about African American citizenship. As pointed out by historian Rayford W. Logan ([1954] 1965),

> So determined were most white Southerners to maintain their own way of life, that they resorted to fraud, intimidation and murder, in order to re-establish their own control of the state governments. They found some justification, in their own eyes at least, in the facts that some Negroes undoubtedly intended to "enjoy their freedom" by taking rest from work . . . Basically, however, the new civil war within the Southern states stemmed from an adamant determination to restore white supremacy. Regulators, Jayhawkers, the Black Horse Cavalry, the Knights of the White Camellia, the Constitutional Union Guards, the Pale Faces, the White Brotherhood, the Council of Safety, the '76

Association, the Rifle Clubs of South Carolina, and, above all, the Ku-Klux Klan terrorized, maimed and killed a large number of Negroes. Not even the presence of federal troops was able to prevent the achievement, by force, of "home rule." In some instances, indeed, Northern soldiers sided with the gangs that terrorized and killed Negroes (21).

Hence, African Americans' experience of slavery, freedom, and citizenship was of an adverse nature. Incident after incident demonstrated to African Americans that whites were not sincere or accommodating in this new relationship, and, therefore, freedom and citizenship did not provide the satisfactions African Americans expected. As African Americans and whites became progressively more incompatible in this new relationship, African Americans learned, and in some instances rediscovered, to dislike, disapprove of, and distrust whites. These feelings did not displace African American expectations but were superimposed upon, and consequently in conflict with, those expectations. African Americans were ambivalent toward whites; whites aroused in them conflicting feelings and thoughts.

Forced to adjust and accommodate themselves, even as children, African Americans experience a paroxysm of shifting emotions involving severe mental anguish and panic. The African American is, therefore, frequently confounded and irked in the realization that color is the decisive social fact of life (Cox [1948] 1970, 383). It is a situation in which African Americans may be distressed and tormented because of their color. As long as race and racism remain prevalent in the society, social crisis is inevitable. It precipitates a situation in which African Americans are mentally tortured by race prejudice.

African Americans have attempted to buttress the psyche through racial socialization, a process begun in slavery. As noted by Grier and Cobbs (1968),

> Every mother, of whatever color and degree of proficiency, knows what the society in which she lives will require of her children. Her basic job is to prepare the child for this. Because of the institutionalization of barriers, the black mother knows even more surely what society requires of her children. What at first seemed a random pattern of mothering has gradually assumed a definite and deliberate, if unconscious, method of preparing [African American children for a] subordinate place in the world (52).

According to sociologist Andrew Billingsley (1992),

> Contemporary African American parents find that they still must teach their children how to manage in a world and community where racial prejudice and discrimination are likely to be aimed against them. It is a harsh reality

which the overwhelming majority of African American parents recognize and for which they seek overtly to prepare their children. Social scientists refer to this practice as "racial socialization." What this means is that black parents recognize the double burden of preparing their children like all other parents to function successfully in society, and in addition, preparing them to function in a society that may often be arrayed against them. They cannot simply be brought up as American children. They must be brought up as American and as black in white America . . . In carrying out this responsibility successfully, parents are called on to function as a buffer between their children and the wider society which is often hostile to them (223-224).

This constitutes a heavy psychological burden that leaves psychological scars. The parent-child relationship will, in general, "reflect the objective cultural conditions of the surrounding social structure" (Freire 1970, 152). As these objective cultural conditions penetrate the home, they are internalized by children, who "either drift into total indifference, alienated from reality by the authorities and myths the latter have used to 'shape' them; or they engage in forms of destructive action" (Freire 1970, 153).

Psychologically emasculated and dependent under slavery, the African American continues to exhibit the inhibitions and psychopathology of the slave experience. It can be argued that the increased incidents of alcohol/substance abuse, homicide, suicide, mental illness, incarceration, domestic violence, and divorce are, in part, casualties of social crisis. The psychological conditions under slavery have not changed very much. Powerful currents larger than the individual experience shape and regulate African American lives far more than white lives. The African American personality and character, as well as their emotions, are determined as much by race as by their personal environment. Every African American is part of a historical legacy that encompasses more than three hundred years. They must expend exceptional psychic energy to soften the blow of learning they are not entitled to what others around them have. Thus, the African American existence encounters unique impediments: discouragement, ostracism, opposition, and hostility. Whereas whites regard their humanity as an ordained right, the African American must struggle for it. They must penetrate barriers and overcome opposition woven into American society that systematically erects obstructions.

Although historically rare among African Americans, suicide is becoming more and more an option for African Americans in crisis. Since the 1980s, African American suicides have witnessed a dramatic increase, particularly among males. Though still below that of whites, African American suicide has become a significant cause of death, after homicides and accidents (Poussaint and Alexander 2000, 12). Several theories have been put forward to explain this phenomenon.

One such theory suggests that the general disequilibrium within society and the disruption of social relations may account for the rise in suicide among African Americans. According to this reasoning, as desegregation advanced and African Americans became more assimilated, the once-uniform status of African Americans as second-class citizens was disrupted by greater freedom, increased mobility, and a new affluence. The incidence of suicide increased as a consequence of the unexpected stresses (Poussaint and Alexander 2000, 55).

Another theory suggests that a sense of fatalism and chronic despair is driving the increase in African American suicide. Factors such as high unemployment rates, shrinking educational opportunities, poverty, crime, drugs, and dwindling government assistance contribute to self-destructive behaviors and suicide (Poussaint and Alexander 2000, 56-58).

Finally, a third explanation posits "victim-precipitated-homicides" as a form of suicide. According to this reasoning, many African Americans, and particularly males, are on a suicidal quest and hence provoke law enforcement authorities or others to kill them (Poussaint and Alexander 2000, 59-60).

All of these explanations may have some limited validity. However, the historical status of African Americans with its attending social adversities still seems the most potent explanation for African American self-destructive behaviors. As pointed out by psychiatrist Alvin Poussaint (2000, 62),

> blacks in America suffer from chronic despair as a reaction to racist oppression, and we know that despair—the loss of hope—is a major risk factor for self-destructive behavior, from the overt act of leaping to one's death or shooting oneself to long-form, indirect suicide through unhealthy lifestyles (excessive drinking, drug abuse, and, in the age of AIDS, risky sexual behavior).

Consequently, when members of a collective experience a social crisis brought on by progressive adversity, they may simultaneously reach the breaking point and, as LaPiere (1954) explains, "adopt a common, rather than individualized, means of resolving the conflict which they have in common" (536). Having rejected some aspect of the status quo (although not necessarily the aspect responsible for the adversity), they adopt some new form of behavior that they expect to satisfy and resolve the conflict. This situation represents a redefinition of the status quo as undesirable and it is abandoned in favor of some new form of behavior.

Social Demoralization

In the complex case of social crisis, the entire system of social control is disrupted; individuals no longer respond to the forces traditionally designed to induce conformity. The social crisis, therefore, constitutes "a factor entering into the determination of the group's morale," jeopardizing the future of the group (LaPiere 1954, 195). Consequently, the social crisis may galvanize group members, providing a basis for unity that ultimately strengthens morale. On the other hand, it may also "shatter the existing morale of the group and lead to utter demoralization" (LaPiere 1954, 196). And when the adversity leading up to social crisis has been prolonged and sustained, a considerable number of group members might find the task of surmounting the crisis as overwhelming. The result is social demoralization: a socio-psychological state in which an undermining of confidence, discipline, and willingness take place, where disorder and confusion reign. Thus corrupted, determination and courage are shaken or destroyed; it is a state of dispiritedness. Random and inconsistent behavior, susceptibility to suggestion by others, and surges of irrelevant action are symptoms of social demoralization. Additionally, the socially demoralized person is very much like the person experiencing depression or mood disorders. The signs and symptoms are similar: anxiety, irritability, impatience, gloominess, negative thinking, hopelessness, meaninglessness, indecisiveness, trouble concentrating, disorientation, memory problems, slowed intellectual functioning, feelings of inadequacy, difficulty communicating, and difficulty controlling anger.

This condition is described by Brazilian educator Paulo Freire (1970, chap.1) as someone submerged in reality, someone who is trapped in a concrete situation unaware of the cause of the condition. Their perception becomes faulty. They are unable to achieve understanding or become aware of what reality is, or at least to interpret reality objectively, uninfluenced by emotion, conjecture, or personal prejudice. If the submersion is deep enough, it may lead to one or more of the following characteristics: (1) fatalism, (2) self-depreciation, (3) dependency, and/or (4) infatuation. So deeply immersed in the situation, the person may interpret his situation as determined by fate, imposed by a supernatural force, spirit, power or God, and hence unchangeable by human intervention. [For an oppressed, demoralized people, religious faith often becomes an antidote to despair; it fills a void and offers hope that the travails of oppression will someday end. So the Christianization of African Americans, to some extent, represents a reaction to, and a consequence of, social demoralization. African American Christians since the antebellum period have tended to expound a brand of Christianity that interprets the African American experience as providential. This particular pattern of African American religious thought has been described by sociologist St. Clair Drake as "Ethiopianism" or "the Ethiopian myth" (Fredrickson 1995, 61). Ethiopianism is derived from the biblical passage in Psalms 68:31, which proclaims that "Princes shall come out of Egypt; Ethiopia shall soon stretch forth her hands unto God." This passage, intellectually and emotionally, provided a narrative structure for African American hopes and aspirations. As an idiom, Ethiopianism certainly encouraged African American social protest either in fraternity with whites or as distinct from whites, as evidenced by the writings and sermons of Robert Alexander Young, David Walker, Henry

Highland Garnet, Edward Blyden, and Alexander Crummell. It served not merely as an outlet, but as an instrument of sanity and self-respect. Nevertheless, this religious faith had very limited effect on African American oppression. The slaves continued to be slaves, the whites continued to be masters, and the cruel, exploitative history wrought by lowly status continued.] Alternatively, such a person submerged in reality becomes self-deprecating, detracting from himself, seeing himself as unworthy, incapable, sinful, wicked, shameful, blameworthy, immoral, and defiled. And this characteristic of self-deprecation is often connected to the first characteristic--fatalism. The person may also become influenced and controlled by something or someone else, thus subordinating himself; he becomes a being-for-another, instead of a being-for-itself. Finally, an impaired person may become infatuated, developing a passionate attraction for, and attachment to, what he has become dependent on.

Philosopher and theologian Cornel West (1993) describes African American social demoralization as nihilism, "the lived experience of coping with a life of horrifying meaninglessness, hopelessness, and (most important) lovelessness" (22-23). It is a disposition of detachment and self-destruction that "breeds a coldhearted, mean-spirited outlook that destroys both the individual and others" (23). This kind of demoralization is angst and "resembles a kind of collective clinical depression . . .under these circumstances black existential angst derives from the lived experience of ontological wounds and emotional scars inflicted by white supremacist beliefs and images permeating U.S. society and culture" (27).

African American social demoralization can also be understood from the perspective of philosopher Martin Heidegger's discussion of Being. Heidegger posits two fundamental modes of existence: authentic existence, in which Being takes possession of its own possibilities, and inauthentic existence, in which possibilities are relinquished or suppressed. Consequently, Being "can either choose itself or lose itself; it can either exist (stand out) as the distinctive being which it is, or it can be submerged in a kind of anonymous routine manner of life, in which its possibilities are taken over and dictated to it by circumstances or by social pressures" (Macquarrie 1968, 14). African American social demoralization is an inauthentic existence because it is devoid of possibilities that have been circumscribed by the social pressure of living in a racially defined society that dictates or suppresses African American possibilities.

Hence, African American social demoralization represents a loss of self. And this loss of self is predicated on how African Americans relate to white Americans. The African American encounter with white America lacks what Heidegger called "authentic solicitude," that is, a personal concern that helps the other to his freedom and to his own unique possibilities for selfhood. Instead, the relation of white Americans to African Americans "is one of indifference or is even an attempt to dominate [them] and to take [their] distinctive existence from [them]" (Macquarrie 1968, 18). African Americans are dominated by a collective white mass whose standards and way of life are imposed upon them, stripping them of the possibilities of choice and compelling them to a uniformity and conformism dictated by the conventions of white society. Hence, between African Americans and white Americans, there is no genuine communication and no authentic Being-with-one-another.

Consequently, the African American experience--or in Heideggerian terms, their Being-in-the-world--discloses itself in the form of moods, which reveal their relationship to the environment. It is the situation in which they find themselves and hence colors their experience. Demoralization is one such mood; it is a state of mind that lights up the situation in which they find themselves. And how African Americans find themselves is partly due to their own choices, but it is also due to choices determined for them by "society or history or heredity or other agencies" (Macquarrie 1968, 21). This means that African Americans must "take over whatever is already given in this particular existence--factors like race, sex, intelligence, emotional stability" (Macquarrie 1968, 21)--into which they have been thrown.

How African Americans understand their experience that is colored by demoralization implies interpretation. In the act of interpretation, meaning is assigned to things. However, meaning is not arbitrarily assigned; it emerges from a prior frame of reference.

Thus, interpretation leads to the question of language and discourse by which Heidegger means "the actual living communication among existents, which gets expressed in language, that is to say, in words and sentences" (Macquarrie 1968, 25). Discourse is expressed through language that "articulates the intelligibility of the world [and] expresses Being-in-the-world" (Macquarrie 1968, 25). Hence, language illuminates the subject matter; it brings expression to what is communicated. But the discourse concerning race actually hides and conceals the matter and obfuscates genuine communication. The discourse concerning race thus degenerates into what "they" (whites) have pre-determined it to be, rather than how it really is. Heidegger describes this as a "falling," deterioration, or a falseness that obscures reality. And the "falling" manifests itself as a tranquillizing that expunges responsibility and anxiety, as alienation that diverts one from authentic selfhood and authentic community, or as scattering in which possibilities are dictated from outside the self.

Hence, African American social demoralization is the situation in which they find themselves, how they experience their Being-in-the-world. Living an inauthentic existence imposed upon them by white society, African Americans have lost themselves, leading to demoralization. This state of mind affects how African Americans understand, interpret, and assign meaning to their experiences. Racial discourse obfuscates the issue of race by hiding and concealing the matter behind disingenuous communication. Hence, the possibilities for an authentic existence are perverted.

Therefore, under such circumstances hope is dashed, and it can only revive from social practice that intervenes in the social crisis and makes social equality possible. In other words, the widespread demoralization among many African Americans is linked to the lack of an ideological framework capable of generating enthusiasm invigorating enough to overcome the crisis-induced state brought on by prolonged social adversity. Enthusiasm is a necessary condition for change, and the lack of enthusiasm among many African Americans can be attributed to the fact that possibilities for movement within society are nearly non-existent. The racial system in America prohibits, if not severely limits, the opportunities for such movement. Consequently, the American racial system has negated any possibility for hope. The realities of inequality and injustice leave no room for the development of enthusiasm. Sapped by racism and injustice, enthusiasm becomes a casualty, hope is lost, and the mind becomes diseased.

Groups may remain in a condition of demoralization for long periods without a systematic outlet. However, according to sociologist Richard T. LaPiere (1954),

> [T]here may, of course, be recurrent but transitory and usually local outburst--e.g., riots, acts of vandalism, and other forms of socially irresponsible conduct. . . . [A]s people suffering from psychological shock are abnormally suggestible and prone to adopt any action pattern that is demonstrated by one of their number, so those who are socially demoralized are abnormally susceptible to control by conversion . . . and they have lost their respect for the authority of many of the traditional offices of the society. They are, at the same time, energized by the tensional by-product of the conflict that is induced by the social crisis. Like people suffering from psychological shock, they must act but have no predetermined course of action (538).

The general demoralization brought on by social crisis provides fertile ground for the growth of new ideologies. It is a time when people may effectively be directed into a given channel of action by conversion. Ideology, here, refers to the structure of ideas or beliefs, including conceptualizations of social causation used as a justification for actions. People demoralized by social crisis generally move away from what they perceive as the cause of the crisis and therefore have "a functional need for a defined course of collective action away from the old and toward some promising alternative [and] a new ideology . . . may offer just such a channel for the release of accumulated tensions" (LaPiere 1954, 540). Consequently, an ideology, which serves to organize the actions of demoralized individuals, will be rebellious in character, it will define the cause of the crisis that stimulated the demoralization, and it will designate a course of action or cure to neutralize the cause of the crisis.

The converts to the new ideology, if induced to overt action, become "a social movement through which the participants discharge their crisis-induced drives to action" (LaPiere 1954, 544). The social movement is supposed to extinguish the causes of social adversity and establish (or reestablish) sources of social satisfactions. But, as LaPiere (1954) explains, "what a social movement does is bring into being a new form of normal social conditions" and controls that reorient participants' conduct, and as the movement evolves "the sense of social crisis dissipates, and with it the demoralization that fostered the rise and acceptance of the ideology on which the movement is based" (544). Participants in the movement are living on futures; however, social movements come to different ends-- success, failure, or disillusionment.

Also, the social movement is one of various types. It may be charismatic, organized around a person. It may be revolutionary, aimed at establishing a new system that provides the satisfactions denied under the old system. Or it may be leaderless and segmental, loosely organized around a central idea and hence determined by the masses. But in general, according the LaPiere (1954),

> [P]eople who have become detached by progressive adversity from the authority of the status quo . . . turn to some other form of authority to provide them guidance. They may generate an ideological basis for action among themselves; more often it is provided for them by some one of their number who is more ingenious and less restrained than the majority. Occasionally they act individually on the basis of this ideology, translating it into action each in his own peculiar way. Far more often, however, they need and secure direction in translating the ideology into action (550).

There are numerous historical examples that demonstrate well African American social demoralization. Slave revolts and conspiracies to revolt were the most desperate reaction to slave status, social adversity, social crisis, and social demoralization. Gabriel Prosser, Denmark Vesey, and Nat Turner are among the better-known examples of violent resistance to slavery, but slave uprisings were prevalent from slavery's onset in America until its abolition in 1865.

The Negro Convention Movement was another device used by free Northern blacks to construct and advocate ideologies not only to fight for abolition but also to pursue independent courses of liberation--sometimes nationalist, sometimes integrationists, and sometimes a combination of the two. Liberation theorists such as Henry Highland Garnet, William Whipper, Samuel Cornish, William Watkins, Alexander Crummell, Frederick Douglass, and Martin Delany were noted participants at these conventions (Stuckey 1987, chap. 4). These conventions met regularly, one of the first meeting in Philadelphia in 1830. Numerous others met in the years preceding the Civil War.

Following Reconstruction, conditions quickly deteriorated for African Americans. As a shift in thinking took place, a cluster of ideologies were proposed to address African Americans' disenfranchisement, political ostracism, inferior education, and lack of economic opportunity. Although characterized as programs for self-help and racial solidarity, these ideologies actually accommodated segregation and discrimination, while they minimized the value of political participation.

In the 20th century, retaliatory and aggressive racial rioting was prevalent: the East St. Louis riot of 1917, the Chicago riot of 1919, the Tulsa riot of 1921, the Detroit riot of 1943, the Harlem riots of 1935 and 1943, the Los Angeles riots of 1965 and 1992, as well as rioting in over 100 cities following Martin Luther King, Jr.'s assassination in 1968. Historians August Meier and Elliot Rudwick (1969) assert,

> [I]t is evident that there have been two major periods of upsurge both in overt discussion by Negro intellectuals concerning the desirability of violent retaliation against white oppressors, and also in dramatic incidents of actual social violence committed by ordinary Negro citizens. One was the period during and immediately after the First World War. The second has been the period of the current civil rights revolution (401).

Meier and Rudwick point out two factors responsible for this contrast in rioting. One has to do with the change in race relations, particularly among African Americans who have raised expectations and become "disillusioned by the relatively slow pace of social change [and become] more restless and militant than before" (406) The second factor is demographic. The Northern migration of African Americans increased their population in major American cities and accentuated the development of vast ghettos; consequently, white mobs were no longer "in a position to chase, beat, and kill isolated Negroes on downtown streets" (406). But given these differences in racial rioting, Meier and Rudwick point out,

> In both periods retaliatory violence accompanied a heightened militancy among American Negroes--militancy described as the "New Negro" in the years after World War I, and described in the sixties, with the phrase, "the Negro Revolt." . . . [I]n both periods a major factor leading Negroes to advocate or adopt such tactics was the gap between Negro aspiration and objective status (407).

Other examples of social demoralization would include the attraction of radical and revolutionary ideologies that fueled organizations such as the Universal Negro Improvement Association, the Nation of Islam, the Black Panther Party, the Revolutionary Action Movement, and the Republic of New Africa. The Universal Negro Improvement Association, founded by Marcus Garvey in 1914, was the first mass-based African American organization. Its ideas of racial pride, separation from whites and white ideas, pride in African heritage, and self-determination were popularized by Garveyites. Marcus Garvey's organization captured the imagination and loyalty of thousands of African Americans as no organization had done before or has done since. It personified the possibilities for African Americans that poverty and prejudice so severely limited (Vincent 1971).

W. D. Fard in Detroit started the Nation of Islam, which emerged from a splintering of the Moorish-American Science Temple founded by Noble Drew Ali, in 1930. His preaching of an unorthodox version of Islam and proclamation that whites were devils and blacks were the original inhabitants of the earth attracted several thousand followers. After his mysterious disappearance in 1934, the leadership passed to Elijah Poole (later Elijah Muhammed), who continued to assert separatism and disdain for whites (Blair 1977).

The Black Panther Party for Self-Defense, founded by Huey P. Newton and Bobby Seale in 1966 in Oakland, California, advocated armed defense of the black community against police brutality. In its ten-point program, the Panthers called for full employment, restitution for slave labor, decent housing, education, exemption from military service, an end to police brutality, freedom for all black prisoners, and a United Nations plebiscite in the black colony for self-determination. Because of its brazen display of black militancy, chapters of the party sprang up in cities across the nation and were hailed as genuine American revolutionaries (Blair 1977).

The Revolutionary Action Movement, organized in Philadelphia around the same time as the Black Panther Party, was a Black Nationalist organization that advocated territorial separation, reparations, and guerrilla warfare. Loosely structured and appealing in many east and west coast cities, the organization was short-lived, thanks to police infiltration and the arrest of its leaders in 1967 (Blair 1977).

Territorial separation was also a central theme of the Republic of New Africa, founded in Detroit in 1967 by Milton Henry (later known as Brother Gaida). Based on the principles of cooperative economics and self-sufficiency, the Republic of New Africa sought to establish a black nation composed of the states of Louisiana, Mississippi, Alabama, Georgia, and South Carolina. According to its leader, the Republic of New Africa would wage military and guerrilla warfare to achieve its aims. The organization was effectively silenced by police and FBI actions (Blair 1977).

Other organizations of note include the revolutionary terrorist groups the Black Liberation Army (BLA) and the Symbionese Liberation Army (SLA). According to Blair, the BLA

> was indicted in 1973 on charges including murder, robbery, grand larceny, and possession of guns. The army's guiding spirit and the leader of the closely knit band that broke from the Black Panther Party in 1971 is said to be Joanne D. Chesimard. The group's membership is small, estimated at one hundred, of whom twenty-five to forty

54

live in the metropolitan New York area, and they are accused of ambushing policemen in New York, St. Louis, North Carolina, and California. Another group, Cinque's . . . the Symbionese Liberation Army, was the most bizarre and smallest revolutionary terrorist group . . . While the twelve-to-twenty-member SLA was on the rampage, it sent shock waves of horror and outrage through the nation, not only because of the armed robberies and violent crimes attributed to it, but by obtaining as a most unlikely recruit the newspaper heiress Patricia Hearst, who was originally kidnapped by the SLA to dramatize their revolutionary goals (Blair 1977, 110-111).

The participation of African Americans in socialist organizations extends back into the early nineteenth century and the very beginnings of organized socialism within the United States. The Communist Club of New York, one of the first communist organizations in the U.S., invited blacks to join as equal members. In 1867, the Communist Club of New York became a section of the International Workingmen's Association, and four years later, African Americans participated in two IWA-sponsored demonstrations in New York (Foner 1977). In 1877, the first African American to identify himself publicly as a socialist emerged: Peter H. Clark, principal of the Colored High School in Cincinnati, former conductor on the Underground Railroad, and one of the editorial managers for Frederick Douglass' North Star (Clark 1942). In 1884, the publication of T. Thomas Fortune's Black and White: Land, Labor and Politics in the South became the first time an African American had argued with such clarity and vigor in favor of African American support for organized labor (Foner 1977). During the 1890s, socialism also appealed to African American ministers. Through two publications of the African Methodist Episcopal Church, African Americans were exposed to socialist ideas, and several ministers later became socialist activists (Foner 1977). Three African Americans were present at the founding of the Socialist Party of America in 1901 (Foner 1977). In 1911, Hubert H. Harrison, an influential member of the Socialist Party's local branch five of Harlem, was given the job of organizing a nucleus organization among African Americans in Harlem, which became the Colored Socialist Club (Foner 1977). During World War I, an impressive group materialized, comprised of young African American and West Indian radicals who were enthusiastic about socialism. A. Philip Randolph and Chandler Owen emerged as two of the most important African American socialists during this period (Foner 1977). Also during this period, the first African American Marxist revolutionary organization in the United States was founded--the African Blood Brotherhood--which later established close ties with the Communist Party (Draper 1960; Grigsby 1987; Kuykendall 2002; Martin 1976).

African Americans also participated in radical labor organizations such as the National Labor Union and its affiliate, the Colored National

Labor Union; the Noble Order of the Knights of Labor; and the American Federation of Labor. These organizations were also heavily influenced by socialists and Marxists (Foner 1974; Kessler 1952).

The modern civil rights movement also fits within this paradigm. Spawned by the landmark case of *Brown v. Board of Education* in 1954, the movement began in Montgomery, Alabama in 1955 when Rosa Parks refused to move to the back of the bus to accommodate a white passenger. This act led to the famous Montgomery bus boycott, which catapulted the movement to national attention. Led by Dr. Martin Luther King, Jr. and a coalition of civil rights groups (including the Southern Christian Leadership Conference, the NAACP, the National Urban League, the Congress of Racial Equality, and the Student Nonviolent Coordinating Committee), the civil rights movement used direct action and civil disobedience to contrast its moral position with the immorality of discrimination and violence against African Americans. Although relatively successful against Southern de jure segregation, the movement began to splinter by the mid-1960s, as African Americans grew increasingly impatient both with the slow progress of racial integration and with white resistance in the form of de facto segregation.

Finally, it may be added that symptomatic of social demoralization are the African American "subcultural pathologies" which include poverty, substandard housing, family disrepute, addictions, weak incentives toward formal education, a slovenly state of physical upkeep, crime, social disorganization, squalor, adult idleness, profanity, neglectful child rearing, and vandalism. The person born into this alienated, racially-ostracized, and unwanted existence is "more or less effectively socialized [into] a system of values, sentiments, and beliefs which makes that class position at least tolerable and, in many instances, all that can be hoped for under the circumstances" (LaPiere 1954, 37). Consequently, when individuals have no control over their experiences, a phenomenon known as "learned helplessness" can precipitate demoralization. In other words, individuals are socialized into demoralization.

The despair that is so prevalent in such an environment produces what is referred to as an "opposition culture": a way of life that opposes the norms of mainstream society. Sociologist Elijah Anderson (1999) describes this oppositional culture as "a product of alienation. It is alluring in large part because the conventional culture is viewed by many blacks in the inner cities as profoundly unreceptive" (287). As a consequence, many African Americans develop contempt for conventional society and its norms, and this contempt helps to legitimize the oppositional culture. As the many social pathologies equated with this oppositional culture become the norm, young people are increasingly socialized into this culture and away from conventional values and behavior.

Consequently, the current state of social demoralization is a process that began for African Americans with slavery. The slave status set in motion a chain of adversities, which ultimately led to social crisis and social demoralization.

Summary

The argument presented thus far is that race relations, in the American context, are status relations. Moreover, they are, specifically, ascribed status relations, making race a determinant of social position. And for African Americans, social position was initially established in slavery and based on a racial designation. The institution of slavery set the tone for race relations in the United States and has firmly defined the status of African Americans for the past several hundred years. Being placed at the very bottom of the social hierarchy meant living on the lowest plane of social existence, which had repercussions on family and child-rearing practices, rendering such practices abnormal in comparison with those of the dominant or mainstream society. This lowly existence also determined the direction of socialization that was not only crucial to African American survival, but also essential for maintaining the social order. The psychological consequences of such a socialization process were devastating for African Americans, both as individuals and as a group. Finally, this entire status system was sustained by governmental policies that both reflected and reinforced the social order.

Additionally, social status was intimately related to social adversity in that it had a bearing on the kinds of and severity of obstacles and frustrations meted out by society. The act of enslavement was an adversity that was both physically and psychologically punishing and tended to find justification in mythical stereotypes that reinforced relations of domination. Also, because the social adversity of slavery affected psychosocial functioning, it tended to engender a degree of pathological suspicion among African Americans. Another consequence of social adversity was that it facilitated the prospects for division among African Americans and invited upon them a type of invasion that corrupted and retarded their thinking. Consequently, prolonged and sustained social adversity affected the state of mind regarding the future of the group and provoked various reactions to change the status quo. However, in the end, social adversity left the mark of oppression that still reverberates within contemporary African American life.

Invariably, progressive social adversity led to a debilitating mental state within African Americans in which hostile internal forces reached a turning point and incompatible psychic forces competed for satisfaction. The social situation became intolerable and unmanageable; thinking became overwhelmed by emotions, and behavior became random and irrelevant, causing cognitive functioning to break down. The social situation was now a social crisis. Precipitated by the social adversities of a lowly status, some African Americans lost faith in the value of traditional social practices, devices, and structures and acquired new values, sentiments, interests, and motivations. Consequently, African Americans developed an array of coping mechanisms not only to reduce and alleviate the tension, but also to protect the self against threats to its integrity. However, the coping mechanisms were, in general, ineffective and maladaptive.

Consequently, while social crisis disrupts social control and may galvanize group members and strengthen morale, it may also shatter morale and lead to social demoralization. When the ability to surmount the social crisis became overwhelming, some African Americans became socially demoralized, undermining confidence, discipline, and willingness. Disorder and confusion became epidemic, perception became faulty, and the susceptibility to conversion to new ideas and beliefs found fertile ground among the demoralized. Social demoralization was expressed in a variety of forms such as social movements, revolts, riots, radical and revolutionary organizations, and subcultural pathologies.

Hence, social status, social adversity, social crisis, and social demoralization are the culmination of a process begun in slavery. Social status is the significant variable, and race relations are really status relations. Hence, status is the primary determinant in situations of race relations.

Therefore, previous explanations (mentioned in the introduction) concerning racial inequality lose sight of the larger context in which race relations take place. All of these explanations have been subjected to substantial critiques. However, a few additional observations are in order.

Deficiency theories erroneously assume that equal opportunities exist for social benefits for all people and that African Americans, because of their own deficiencies, are incapable of seizing or are unqualified to seize the opportunities. Consequently, African Americans are responsible for their own victimization. This absurd kind of thinking, in its attempt to justify racial inequality, completely disregards the clear and persistent historical record of the lack of equal opportunity. African Americans were rarely, if ever, given opportunities of the kind or quality reserved for whites. Furthermore, because of their status, African Americans were not in a position to compete effectively or fairly for whatever opportunities were available. African Americans were systematically deprived of the requisite social, political, cultural, and economic tools necessary to gain social advantages; even when those African Americans had the requisite tools they were not given adequate opportunities to use those advantages.

Bias theories, on the other hand, only make a case for the consequences of racial prejudice and discrimination. Bias theories lack tangible explanations for what actually causes racial prejudice and whether there are psychosocial and cultural components to which racial prejudice is indebted. Answers to these questions would enhance the explanatory power of bias theories and give them a comprehensiveness they currently lack. Therefore, an understanding of social status places racial prejudice within a larger social context from which to gauge its psychosocial and cultural origins and effects.

Finally, structural theories give too much significance to economics in explaining racial inequality. Political scientist Cedric J. Robinson (1983) presents an interesting challenge to structural theories, particularly Marxist theories, by asserting racialism is endemic to Western culture and runs deep in the bowels of Western civilization. Thus the phenomenon of race relations must be pursued first in intra-European racialism and the effects it had on European consciousness. According to Robinson, "Western culture, constituting the structure from which European consciousness was appropriated, the structure in which social identities and perceptions were grounded in the past, transmitted a racialism which adapted to the political and material exigencies of the moment" (82). If Robinson is correct, then racism is not a consequence of capitalism or economic organization, but is actually a piece of the process that contributed to the organization of capitalism.

The foregoing theories are also problematic because they are single-variable explanations, and behavior is almost never determined by a single variable, but rather sets of factors. Whether we accept genetic inheritance, cultural traits, prejudice, or economic organization as causal factors in African American behavior, they are interdependent, rather than independent, variables. These factors enter into the complex interaction of personality and environment, out of which conduct emerges. These differentials are so blended and interwoven that, however sophisticated the explanation, no single variable can possibly explain why individuals act under certain circumstances in the ways they do.

Also, all these explanations seem to focus on race as the causal factor (or at least a significant one). But race cannot be the cause of dysfunctionality, and neither can social dysfunctionality be the exclusive effect of race. Following a line of reasoning by Reverend Hosea Easton in "A Treatise on the Intellectual Character, and Civil and Political Condition of the Colored People of the United States" (1969), if race were the sole cause of social dysfunctionality, then as the cause varies, so does the effect. That is, each racial group would be subject to particular social dysfunctions exclusive to that group. But it is well known that the same or similar intellectual deficiencies and abnormal or deviant cultural traits can be found among all racial groups, not just African Americans.

Furthermore, if social dysfunctionality is the exclusive effect of racism, then race is an independent variable capable of acting on its own. It must have configurative properties independent of social attitudes. If that is the case then why can we not comprehend its existence outside of social situations? Since this cannot be done, then race cannot be regarded as anything other than a passive principle in which there is no power of action.

Now, this is not to say that these explanations lack some elements of the truth, because they do call attention to specific problems among African Americans. However, their value is not as single, independent explanations but as interdependent explanations. Because African Americans began as slaves and continued as second-class citizens, cultural deficiencies were forced upon their population and made endemic. The adversity of slavery and the bipartite system degraded and humiliated African Americans to the point of cultural retardation. Also, the system of slavery and the bipartite system were predicated on racial prejudice and discrimination. Racism has been responsible for all the factors that perpetuate African American social demoralization: myths, conformity to domination, division, cultural invasion, and stigmatization. Furthermore, the U.S. economic organization during slavery and the bipartite system placed the African American at an economic disadvantage, which was maintained through racism and exacerbated by social adversity. Additionally, the accumulated effects of lowly status and social adversity engendered a social crisis in which African Americans were psychologically emasculated and which enhanced, or otherwise intensified, social disorganization and economic dislocation. And as the effects of social crisis degenerated into social demoralization, African Americans sought alternative political and economic solutions, as well as engaged in counter-cultural behavior as a means of either alleviating the effects of a harmful environment or changing the nature of the environment. Therefore, deficiency theories, bias theories, and structural theories are given greater depth of meaning when understood within the context of social status. These theories become viable supporting explanations (rather than single explanations by themselves) in interpreting the effects of lowly social status.

Understandably, the preceding discussion of race relations will generate some objections, which I will try to address. One objection might be that I have simply presented a modified version of the caste-class model of race relations. But the caste-class model is static and assumes the parties involved in the social relations acknowledge and accept their positions as legitimate. The model that I present is dynamic; it recognizes that racial inequality is imposed on African Americans rather than accepted as legitimate, and it accounts for changes in social relations and mobility within the status gradient.

A second objection might be that my explanation also suffers from a single variable explanation-- that I deduce the consequences of race relations from social status. Although I propose social status as a primary determinant of individual behavior, I acknowledge its interdependent nature. Social status does not emerge in isolation from other social phenomena, and this is true particularly in the case of African Americans, where cultural, economic, political, and religious variables have played a significant role in establishing status. Furthermore, social status is a starting point and is by no means used as a final determinant of behavior. Social status is only used as a first premise to which other propositions are linked and conclusions drawn.

A third objection might be that I have focused almost exclusively on the consequences of race relations for African Americans, and I have demonstrated little, if any, insight into race relations from the white American perspective. This I would say is a valid criticism. My intent, however, is not to put forward some grand explanation of race relations; rather, I want to examine the consequences of American race relations on the subjugated race, which is in this case African Americans. My purpose is to provide some additional insight into African American social behavior, so often portrayed as lacking positive or affirmative qualities, by proposing an explanation that could reveal its socio-psychological reasons without being an indictment or critique of it.

A final objection, more ideological in nature, might be that I have presented an excuse to bolster African American victimization that relinquishes them from individual responsibility. However, the evidence I have presented demonstrates that African Americans have been, and remain, victimized by American race relations. I believe I have presented considerable support that attests to the harm, injury, loss, and even death suffered by African Americans as a consequence of race relations. I have also shown that African Americans have taken the initiative to change their status, although not always in the most rational and responsible way. Because the consequences of lowly status are in part emotive, there will be individual variation in how some persons react, and my explanation has taken this into consideration under the topics of "social crisis" and "social demoralization."

Finally, it must be added that the virulence of racism is still as strong as ever. Racist militia and paramilitary groups are sprouting up across America, espousing racial paranoia and hatred. The Southern Poverty Law Center (2002) identified 708 active hate groups in 2002 and estimates that over 50,000 hate crimes occur each year in the United States. These organizations exist in practically every state in the nation, the majority located in the Midwest and in the northeast and southern states.

Also, racism is maintained as much by corporate managers and executives "as by hood-wearing white hoodlums" (Rowan 1996, 20). Numerous investigative reporters have demonstrated "the fact that even a black person of exceptional prestige and large financial resources has a more difficult time of getting a housing loan than a white applicant with lesser qualifications" (Rowan 1996, 20). One can also find among "corporate boardrooms, local governments, education districts . . . powerful men and women who are virulent bigots but will become stridently indignant and threaten to sue if someone calls them racist. So racism thrives, safe behind a curtain of politically correct language" (Rowan 1996, 22-23).

Politicians also continue to appeal to racism to win elections and push racist agendas. Beginning in 1968, the Republican Party employed its "southern strategy" designed to siphon white, southern Democrats into the Republican Party by convincing them that the Democratic party had abandoned them in favor of African Americans. Ronald Reagan helped to widen that wedge and make white racism both tolerable and fashionable in national politics again. In September 1980, the Invisible Empire Knights of the Ku Klux Klan declared in its newspaper "Reagan its favorite candidate, asserting that the Republican platform reads as if it were written by a Klansmen" (Rowan 1996, 56). In 1988, George Bush played the race card by displaying Willie Horton, an African American convict who committed murder while involved in a convict release program, as personifying everything that is wrong with the Democratic party and society in general. During the contested presidential election in 2000, African American voters in Florida were intimidated from going to the polls, were denied the right to vote, and were systematically removed from the voter rolls. In 2002, Trent Lott, Republican U.S. Senator from Mississippi, heaped praise upon retiring South Carolina Senator Strom Thurmond (an avowed racist and Dixiecrat candidate for president in 1948) saying the country would be better off had Thurmond won the presidency. In that same year, the Georgia gubernatorial election was waged over a proposal to revise the state flag to make the confederate emblem more prominent. This battle was also previously waged in the states of South Carolina and Mississippi.

In August 2002, the United Nations Committee on the Elimination of Racial Discrimination expressed concern about the United States' failure to live up to the provisions of the Convention on the Elimination of All Forms of Racial Discrimination. The committee highlighted concerns about police brutality, the disproportionately high incarceration rates of African Americans and Hispanics, unequal treatment in the criminal justice system; racial disparities in the application of the death penalty; disenfranchisement of minorities after they have served criminal sentences; mistreatment of indigenous peoples; and continuing racial discrimination and disparities in housing, employment, education, and health care. The committee also noted the dismissiveness of the United States' response to these concerns and its insistence that racial discrimination is not a problem, although it provided no data to support this contention (Human Rights Watch 2002).

In September 2002, the United States withdrew its delegation from the United Nations World Conference Against Racism, Racial Discrimination, Xenophobia and Related Intolerance in Durban, South Africa, citing concerns about references to Zionism. However, the Bush Administration was also uneasy about references to reparations for slavery and other forms of racial discrimination in the United States (Human Rights Watch 2002).

Given the psychosocial effects of racism, is it possible that racism is a mental illness? This issue was first raised during the civil rights era of the 1960s by African American psychiatrists, who proposed to the American Psychiatric Association that extreme racism be classified as a diagnosable mental illness. The Association declined to recognize racism as a mental illness, arguing that racism is a cultural problem and not a personal pathology. But Dr. Alvin Poussaint, who was among those African American psychiatrists during the 1960s, believes it is time to reconsider racism as a diagnosable mental illness. According to Poussaint, "extreme racism is a serious mental illness [and] meets criteria for a paranoid 'delusional disorder,' a major psychiatric illness included in the Diagnostic and Statistical Manual of Mental Disorders" (Poussaint and Alexander 2000, 125). Poussaint has a valid argument with regard to the case of extreme racism, and it might be further argued that racism is a manifestation of "shared psychotic disorder," a delusional system in which significant numbers of white Americans participate. However, it must be realized that racism is a social construction that serves a social function: to justify and maintain status relations within the social status gradient and preserve white privilege.

CHAPTER TWO

Race Relations and the Meaning of American Nationhood

Therefore, without question the racial problem has been and remains at the center of contention about the meaning of American nationhood. In <u>Democracy in America</u>, Alexis de Tocqueville writes, "[T]he most formidable evil threatening the future of the United States is the presence of blacks on their soil. From whatever angle one sets out to inquire into the present embarrassment or future dangers facing the United States, one is always brought up against this basic fact" (1969, 340). These words speak to the problem of racial inclusion, and specifically African American incorporation into American society, that still remains today.

Politically, American society is organized around race. Race is, without exaggeration, the biggest issue and concern in American politics. I think this statement is justifiable on the grounds that white Americans were willing during the Civil War to slaughter each other over how dark-skinned people of African descent should live. Its political prominence is so great because it stimulates and marshals Americans around emotional territory that is deep and extreme within the social life of the nation. Commenting on the racial divide in the 1984 presidential election, political scientists Robert Huckfeldt and Carol Kohfeld (1989) found the racial polarization "unequaled by any other social boundaries" (1). They further comment that despite political differences between rich and poor, educated and uneducated, working class and middle class, "the politics of race has emerged as the most meaningful boundary in American politics . . ." (1).

The economic picture is no different. African American income remains significantly below that of whites, and African American unemployment remains significantly higher than that of whites. Although the economic picture is much more complex to interpret, the point is that status, when combined with race, is very significant in terms of who works where, of being employed, or being in poverty.

And socially, the strong impulse remains towards exclusion, racial isolation, and racial segregation in neighborhoods, schools, work environments, and communities. The idea of community "encapsulates a powerful racial imagery" (Prager 1987, 66).

In the 1980s, a significant body of communitarian literature emerged (Bellah et al. 1985; Gelp 1989; Kamenka 1982; Miami Theory Collective 1991). In general, the communitarian literature called into question liberal individualism, to which it attributed modern social problems and in particular the detached, dislocated self. Communitarian theorists proposed as a solution a return to community values and traditions that situate the individual; reconnect the individual with a past; and give the individual life identity, meaning, and purpose. Yet, despite the persistence of racial exclusion, racial division, and racial discrimination in American society, communitarian theorists were essentially silent about the racial problem.

This omission by communitarian theorists is a glaring example showing that white Americans have never perceived persons of African descent in America as truly part of the American community. Perhaps this is because persons of African descent entered America not as persons but as property, which Herbert Hill (1985) points out as one of the peculiar ironies about slavery in the United States: "Although slaves were not legally recognized as persons, central to the institution of slavery was the requirement that these less-than-human chattels, or 'articles of commerce' (by legal definition), perform one of the most creative of human tasks: work" (1). Hence, the idea that white Americans have of African Americans is mediated by the social context of slavery, and this idea, according to social scientist Barbara Fields (1982), "remains true even when time-honored tradition provides a vocabulary for thinking and talking about the other people that runs counter to immediate experience" (149).

Given this history, race is a collective or social representation. In other words, "the racial problem is a function of the American inability to experience blacks in the same way as other members of the political community" (Prager 1987, 75). Another way of understanding this is by way of what psychiatrist Ronald Laing (1967) refers to as scandal networks:

> The members of a scandal network may be unified by ideas to which no one will admit in his own person. Each person is thinking of what he thinks the other thinks. Each person does

not mind [an African American] lodger, but each person's
neighbor does. Each person, however, is a neighbor of his
neighbor. What they think is held with conviction. . . . The
scandal group is a series of others which each serial number
repudiates in himself (53-54).

What is apparent in this situation, continues Laing, is the formation of a
"we" and "they" distinction, in which "We come into being as a group
[where] it is necessary not only that I regard, let us say, you and him and
me as We, but that you and he also think of us as We" (56). So quite
simply, the racial problem in America is a "we" and "they" distinction
in which the white American "we" see the African American "they" as
neither with nor part of them.

Now this relates to communitarian literature from the angle
that this literature argues from a white perspective. Sociologist Robert
Bellah (1985) and his co-authors, for example, focus on, and get their data
from, white, middle-class Americans. The book represents white ethnic
diversity, but not racial diversity. This implies that whites constitute
Americans, and that non-whites are insignificant as far as American
culture is concerned. It demonstrates that white ethnics are assimilable.
Therefore, it becomes problematic, if not pointless, to discuss the racial
problem in communitarian terms if African Americans are not perceived as
assimilable or part of the American community.

However, this last statement should not be mistaken for a defense
of communitarian literature's silence on the racial problem. It is merely
an interpretation based on the historical experience of African American
exclusion from the American community with a socio-psychological
explanation for that exclusion which could perhaps account for
communitarian literature's silence on the racial problem.

The white perspective that communitarian literature takes might
also be premised on the understanding that liberal individualism is a
European and Euro-American phenomenon. Bellah (1985) and his co-
authors explicitly state that their data comes from white, middle-class
Americans, and Carl Starkloff (1989) is even more candid when he says,
"As an ethos, individualism typifies white middle-class Americans" (157).
Alasdair MacIntyre (1984) and Charles Taylor (1984) reach back to the
European Enlightenment to make their argument. The point, however, is
not the European ancestry of liberal individualism. Liberalism was indeed
a product of the European Renaissance and Reformation, but since the
communitarian literature criticizes liberal individualism, it is, in essence,
criticizing a European mind-set. Therefore, to discuss the racial problem
within the context of liberal individualism would be to discuss something
not necessarily connected to liberal individualism.

Another explanation concerning communitarian literature's
silence on the racial problem might very well have to do with a general
silence about the problem in society at-large. Following the civil rights
movement, a public restraint was placed on racial language. Even among

social scientists, according to sociologist William J. Wilson (1987), there was the inclination to avoid "researching behavior construed as unflattering or stigmatizing to racial minorities" (4). So discussion now uses other categories to distinguish the deserving from the undeserving. In particular, the new emphasis on class has tended to deflect attention away from the significance of race. For example, William J. Wilson's very influential book, The Declining Significance of Race (1978), argues race relations directly reflect relations of economic and political power. In the antebellum period, race determined the status of African Americans; in the late nineteenth and early twentieth century, race and class characteristics interacted; and, in the current era, race has declined in significance. Thus, Williams argues, the problems usually associated with race are no longer a function of racism but exclusively a function of class position.

With regard to communitarian literature's silence on the racial problem, this explanation is purely speculative. However, it should not be overlooked as an explanation. Perhaps communitarian theorists, like many other social scientists, believe that to focus on race is to limit any argument seeking to explain the problems of societal organization.

Historically, the racial problem has been a central feature of American life, and it without question engages a debate about the meaning of American nationhood: Who is included? Who is excluded? How are relationships defined? What kind of political community does America aspire to? How can this aspiration be achieved? The racial problem is a reflection of America's encounter with itself. As pointed out by social scientist Jeffrey Prager (1987), the African American experience is unique, since African Americans have "neither integrated as equal members of the political community, nor ignored or excluded as outsiders, have served as a lightening rod for American self-examination" (63). As such, African Americans become "the measure of American achievement, the test of self-proclaimed principles, the affirmation of self-understanding" (63). The racial problem presents itself as America's greatest democratic challenge and is central to an articulation of citizenship. The exclusion of African Americans from the American community has proved problematic to the pursuit of a "more perfect union." As a consequence, according to social scientist Donald Robinson (1971),

> [there] could be no escape for any American from the consequences of the sins of discrimination and exploitation committed by whites against blacks. And the problem that began in the founding period could not be settled until the American people, the whole American people, undertook the work of reconciliation to which their Declaration of Independence committed them from the outset (446).

Thus, the racial problem enters the communitarian debate by way of history. But it can also be introduced by way of moral discourse. In his critically acclaimed book, An American Dilemma (1944), Gunnar

66

Myrdal conceives of race relations in the United States as a moral issue, and his investigation is an examination of morals. The non-violent and Christian element of the civil rights movement framed its demands in moral language.

Some communitarian literature also frames the debate in terms of morality. Alasdair MacIntyre's 1984 book, in which the predominant theme is the state of disorder found in the language of morality, bears the subtitle "A Study in Moral Theory." Robert Bellah (1985) and his co-authors also were interested in the connection between morality and political community. Hence, the racial problem can be framed in moral language and reconstructed within the historical narrative since communities persist, and indeed require, "standards of right and wrong that one can count on and that are not subject of incessant renegotiation" (Bellah et al, 1985, 140).

Finally, the racial problem could be introduced into the communitarian debate by way of the critique of individualism, which states that the individual is responsible to the self and no one else. Self-reliant individuals are preoccupied with occupational and economic aims. This kind of utilitarian thinking defines the individual and his relation to the community. Thus, those who fail--the needy and the dependent--are responsible for their own failure and are hence peripheral to the main concerns of the community: self-reliance and self-support. In this light, the silence about the racial problem is not surprising, nor is the resentment concerning the resources directed to those incapable of self-support. Some see the racial problem as a problem of economic opportunity in which the community's role, as well as that of the government, is limited in the promotion of this objective. Those who do not fit the economic mold are conceived of as a public menace, unable to be affected by "good works," and therefore they defy the possibility of being included in the American community.

Hence, the racial problem could be introduced into the communitarian debate by way of history, moral discourse, or the critique of individualism. And if real communities are, as Robert Bellah (1985) and his co-authors claim, "communities of memory" (153)--communities with a history--then African Americans are undeniably linked to that past; they are part of its constitutive narrative. And though unpleasant and tragic as the African American role is in this narrative, "[a] genuine community of memory will also tell painful stories . . . And if the community is completely honest, it will remember stories not only of suffering received but of suffering inflicted--dangerous memories, for they call the community to alter ancient evils" (Bellah et al 1985, 153). To deny this past, with its "dangerous memories," its debts, and its inheritances, is to deform the entire notion of community and human relationships.

The African American relationship to the political community is also generally ignored or neglected, particularly within the field of political science. In the area of political culture studies, African American respondents are either treated as statistically insignificant or their political culture is ignored, denied, or treated as pathological. Studies dealing with political socialization generally compare African American political socialization with white political socialization. Usually, they find African Americans lagging behind whites in terms of political knowledge, efficaciousness, and trust in the political system. In the area of African American political opinion, the research suggests that African American political opinion is either baseless or out of line with white opinions and is thus impotent. African American voting behavior has generally been reduced to socio-economic indexes, fear and apathy, and group consciousness. Studies of African American party behavior have generally established a Democratic bias, based on socio-economic variables. And finally, in the area of international political behavior, African Americans are rarely studied or included as forces or actors. In general, according to political scientist Hanes Walton, Jr. (1985), African American political behavior is portrayed as dysfunctional; consequently, this tendency to render African Americans outside the mainstream political system and "invisible is part of a broader pattern in race relations, and must be seen and understood in that larger context" (xxi).

Therefore, just as with their lowly social status, African Americans have had to struggle against their lowly political status. Just as they have been marginalized within the socio-economic structure, so have they been marginalized within the political community. The very beliefs, arguments, and processes that relegated African Americans to the bottom of the social structure have also been used to keep them outside or on the fringes of the political community. The lowly status accorded African Americans, based on a deep-rooted racism, has not only sustained the subordinate-superordinate structure of American society, but has also significantly accorded African Americans their place in the political system. Although efficient, slavery was not indispensable to the preservation of African American subordination. Though significant changes have occurred over the many years and though "the more visibly offensive aspects of this subordination have been gradually removed, the basic subordinate-superordinate structure remains" (Morris 1992, 584).

At the very birth of the American nation, the much-romanticized American Revolution did little, if anything, toward altering the social thinking, values, and institutions prevalent during the colonial era. As pointed out by political scientist Milton Morris (1992), "It is not surprising, therefore, that such a revolution left a culture of religious bigotry and racism intact, and that its principle document [U.S. Declaration of Independence] served as a document to which people referred vaguely, without a need to fully implement its principles" (586). Concepts such as liberty and equality had little influence on the new political system. Instead, as pointed out by Morris (1992), "political values were formulated and articulated in such a manner as to ensure continued black subordination" (587).

As popular democracy gained acceptance during the Jacksonian era of the nineteenth century, it brought no immediate benefit for African Americans, whether enslaved or free. Commitment to mass political participation coexisted with African American subordination. Historian Carl Degler observed that not only were African Americans excluded from political participation, but that the form of this new popular democracy operated to African American disadvantage. According to Degler, as the demand for political equality and participation increased among whites, the need to further subjugate and dehumanize African Americans also increased. As the white masses entered the political arena, they vigorously resisted what they perceived as a threat to their new status-- that is, African American competition--and so "new cognizance was given in both society and politics to the wishes and prejudices of the common [white] man" (Morris 1992, 591). Following the Civil War, historian C. Vann Woodward asserts that "political democracy for the white man and racial discrimination for the black were often products of the same dynamics" and that "the barriers of racial discrimination mounted in direct ratio with the tide of political democracy among whites" (Morris 1992, 591). Thus, Morris (1992) concludes that "democratic values held by Americans have not been a significant hindrance to the institutionalization of racism . . . 'Popular democracy' has been the hand-maiden of racism in the United States because of the absence of such values [that is, values of inclusiveness on equal terms]" (591).

The federal system has also been used as a bulwark against African American inclusion within the political community. First, federalism left African American status largely within state jurisdictions. As a result, states were given complete discretion in managing the institution of slavery and the social and economic condition of African Americans. Federalism has also been significant in obstructing efforts toward social and political change, such as when "the national government attempted to respond to vital needs of blacks either by legislative or judicial action, the rights and prerogatives of the states have been invoked to obstruct national effort" (Morris 1992, 593). Even though the states' rights argument has lost most of its influence, federalism as a system maintains "a special set of weapons for resistance in the form of countless legal, constitutional and administrative devices that can long delay and sometimes defeat a detested national decision" Morris 1992, 594).

Even as they were excluded from the body politic, African Americans struggled for political power because, as pointed out by historians Mary F. Berry and John W. Blassingame (1992),

> [T]hey believed it would end racial discrimination and ultimately result in improved economic and social conditions in the black community. Beyond the usual rewards of political action in a democratic system--patronage, influence on domestic and foreign policy, and access to decision makers--they expected better jobs, better education, and ultimately equal status with whites in the society. They believed political participation would free white Americans from bondage to the practices of racism and inequality and

would liberate blacks from their oppression (598).

Hence, as persistently as whites have denied African Americans their political rights, African Americans have persistently and passionately struggled to obtain them.

Before the Civil War, free African Americans attempted to win the franchise by appealing to whites through petitions, periodicals, and state and national conventions. They contended that disfranchisement was immoral, undemocratic, and tyrannical and so appealed to "whites to vote for men of principle, free the slaves, enfranchise blacks, and to see clearly the distinction between political and social equality" (Berry and Blassingame 1992, 599). And during Reconstruction, when martial law was imposed on the South and Congress disfranchised many of the rebels, African American participants in state conventions to draw up new constitutions refused to disfranchise whites that supported the confederacy (Berry and Blassingame 1992, 603). Hence, during Reconstruction, African Americans began to obtain some of the traditional fruits of political participation. But such participation was short-lived. After 1877, African American political participation "became increasingly fraught with dangerous consequences," as legal measures were implemented to permanently disenfranchise African Americans, so that by 1889 "blacks had been practically eliminated from Southern politics" (Berry and Blassingame 1992, 606).

But African Americans continued the struggle for political rights. Through the convention movement, African Americans emphasized political rights to end Jim Crow and lynching, and with the establishment of the National Association for the Advancement of Colored People (NAACP), African Americans pursued civil and political rights through the courts and Congress. After the African American migration north, they made some limited headway by participating in local, machine-style politics. However, it was not until African Americans shifted their support to the Democratic Party in the 1930s and 40s that they attained some political relief, opening the door to the civil rights movement, which ultimately ushered in a new wave of African American political participation and what has been called the "second Reconstruction."

However, with more African American political participation than ever before, many African Americans began to realize the limits of suffrage. The continuing problems of unemployment, inferior schools, poverty, and accusations by whites of reverse discrimination demonstrated to African Americans that they "could not, even with a few white allies, vote the nation into a benevolent democracy" (Berry and Blassingame 1992, 630). The fundamental changes (both in the economic system and in the deep-rooted, racist beliefs of many whites) necessary to improve the status of the African American masses seemed impervious to any amount of political participation. Consequently, African Americans still remain on the fringes of the political community. Although much more visible on the political stage, African Americans remain relative outsiders in terms of political influence. Because they lack adequate representation, resources, and access, African Americans find their interests are generally ignored or compromised.

By way of conclusion, let me make three points about the silence on the racial problem and the consequences of that silence. First, this silence represents the assumption that the United States was conceived as, and therefore is, an all-white nation. Given the history of race relations in America-- the beliefs, prejudices, and sentiments-- the racial situation seems to indicate the truth of this assumption. When whites think of themselves in relation to African Americans (or any non-white group of people), as pointed out by social psychologists Kenneth Clark (1965), "[whites] need not appraise [their] own strengths and weaknesses, but enjoy membership in a homogeneous and superior white group in which ethnic and class differences are erased" (228). But for the African American, regardless of whether he wears the white man's clothes, eats the white man's food, speaks the white man's language, or professes the white man's religion, he is unable to be a WASP. African Americans are unable to forget the past, because the past lives in their epidermal coloration; they are unable to climb upwards into an elite culture, because the epidermal coloration cannot fade with upward mobility.

Consequently, African Americans are unattached elements within the polity. And as unattached and alienated elements, African Americans' confidence and trust in America and its government is much lower than any other racial or ethnic group in America. Their personal sense of civic competence and efficacy is difficult to maintain within a sea of discouragement; their sense of hope is dashed with each insult to their humanity.

Second, and related to the first point, African Americans are invisible. I think no one has made this any clearer than novelist Ralph Ellison ([1947] 1972), who in a brilliant novel captured the essence of what it is like to go through life unrecognized, unacknowledged: "I am invisible, understand, simply because people refuse to see me . . . When they approach me they see only my surroundings, themselves, or figments of their imagination--indeed, everything and anything except me" (3). This refusal of whites to recognize African Americans creates resentment and anger. Consequently, notes Ellison, "[you] ache with the need to convince yourself that you do exist in the real world, that you're part of all the sound and anguish, and you strike out with your fist, you curse and you swear to make them recognize you. And, alas, it's seldom successful" (4). So having either no outlet or inappropriate outlets, African Americans are almost always in an emotional tight-grip: wound-up, tensed, and angry. And sometimes, after sustaining all the insults, the emotional flood breaks loose.

Thus, this invisibleness engenders silence. And, consequently, there is a deep-seated resistance among whites against the racial problem being presented in all its hideous fullness, in all of the totality of its meaning. As a result, many white Americans speak and think about the race problem in ways that remove them from complicity in the system of racial inequality. As described by psychologist William Ryan (1971), whites "are, most crucially, rejecting the possibility of blaming, not the victims, but themselves. They are all unconsciously passing judgments on themselves and bringing in a unanimous verdict of Not Guilty" (28). Consequently, as explained by sociologist David T. Wellman (1977), white Americans can "be conscious of inequality and injustice without condemning themselves . . . recognize a societal problem without implicating the society, and . . . defend their interests without referring to genes or race" (221). How is this possible? Because, asserts Wellman, "they recognize racial inequality either abstractly or as blocked access; they explain it in terms of the problems of its victims; and they 'solve' the problem with solutions that do not affect white people" (221). In fact, according to Wellman, what whites propose as solutions to the race problem "are not, in any basic sense, 'solutions' for black people." Instead, "the solutions allow white people to recognize the need for change without having that change affect them in important ways;" so, "they get off the hook and defend their racial privilege as well" (221).

Hence, white privilege is gained from African Americans' disadvantages, and whites cannot (or will not) tolerate the idea of diminishing white privilege to improve African Americans' status. Therefore, white privilege as the corollary of racism is denied, and white privilege is protected from being fully acknowledged, lessened, or ended.

Now what white privilege amounts to, according to Women's Studies professor Peggy McIntosh (1988), is "an invisible package of unearned assets that I can count on cashing in each day . . . [it] is like an invisible weightless knapsack of special provisions, maps, passports, codebooks, visas, clothes, tools, and blank checks" (1). White privileges are conditions attached to skin color regardless of class, religion, ethnic status, or geographical location, and on which African Americans cannot count. And these conditions work to systematically over-empower whites by conferring dominance because of race.

To acknowledge white privilege would mean giving up the myth of meritocracy, the myth that this is a free country, the myth that one's life is what one makes of it. Instead, as pointed out by McIntosh (1988), "whiteness protected me from many kinds of hostility, distress, and violence, which I was being subtly trained to visit in turn upon people of color" (3). Therefore, unearned white privilege confers power that looks "like strength when it is in fact permission to escape or to dominate" (McIntosh 1988, 3). The silences and denials surrounding white privilege "keep the thinking about equality and equity incomplete, protecting unearned advantage and conferred dominance by making these taboo subjects" (McIntosh 1988, 4).

The invisibleness of the African American extends back to the nation's founding. The Founding Fathers, framers of the U.S. Constitution, really conceived of an all-white nation, no matter the absurdity of this position, given the presence of Africans and Native Americans in the colonies. Africans in America, as well as Native Americans, were simply an adjunct, casually written into the body politic as non-persons without civil rights. Consequently, the Bill of Rights and the Civil War Amendments have proven insufficient and unreliable as protections for African Americans and as guarantees of economic, political, or cultural equality.

So what is going on here is the defense of American ideals. White Americans are exonerated, and America is legitimated. America has been good to white people, and whether racism is intentional or consequential, it insures the continuation of white privilege and the racial status quo. Perhaps journalist Samuel F. Yette (1975) was right when he asserted African Americans are obsolete people who have outlived their usefulness. No longer an economic asset, they have become an economic liability: "The wood is all hewn, the water all drawn, the cotton all picked, and the rails reach from coast to coast. The ditches are all dug, the dishes are put away, and only a few shoes remain to be shined" (14). And so, the race problem quietly loses its sense of urgency. "Always denied social value," says Yette, African Americans have "also lost economic value," and "their raison d'etre to this society has ceased to be a compelling issue" (14).

Third and finally, this silence appears an admission of innocence on the part of white Americans; it appears a denial of responsibility for their part in creating and sustaining the racial problem. It is an attempt by whites to cut themselves off from that past which lives in the present, a past built upon a historical deed of wrong against African Americans, a past fraught with tragic consequences as to make them not want to look at it or think of it. It is a refusal to understand how subtly and yet strongly African Americans are linked to the life and fate of the American community. Consequently, this collective guiltlessness reinforces the sense of detachment and alienation. It bolsters the insults and deepens the discouragement; it amplifies the awareness of invisibility. In short, it perpetuates the racial problem.

CHAPTER THREE

Political Class Struggle and the Race Problem

Each phase of the African American experience--lowly status, social adversity, social crisis, and social demoralization--has engendered reactions. The responses to the race problem have been highlighted throughout this discussion and included a vast array of group and individual reactions: self-and-group-destructive behavioral patterns, adhesion and identification with the oppressor, resentment and hatred, "bad conscience," "cultural paranoia," passing and shuttling, self-help associations, protests, demonstrations, boycotts, appeals, racial socialization, and demoralization. However, the reactions have tended to be responses to the immediate consequences of racial antagonism, such as enslavement, segregation, racism, and disparities in social, economic, and political resources. In other words, the responses have, in general, been stimulated by social adversity, a direct consequence of social status. But in large measure the responses have been toward symptoms of the African American condition, and symptoms are not causes.

Nevertheless, this is understandable. So immersed in the concrete situation of oppression, African Americans are unaware of the causes of the condition. Their perception is faulty; their understanding and interpretation of oppression lacks objectivity. Unable to perceive the reality of oppression as a limiting situation that can be objectively verified, they remain prey to its force.

So, the race problem really is not an issue about cultural deficiency, racial bias, or structural dislocation. The race problem is an issue of power. And social power, as defined by social psychologist Kenneth B. Clark

(1974), involves the necessary energy "to create, to sustain, or to prevent social change" (76). Since the race problem is conditioned by status, and because status determines one's relationship to power, then problems of race are really problems that revolve around power. A person's status is a direct reflection of his power in the world. How a person lives, where and in what condition he lives, how he will by reared and socialized, the extent of psychological suffering, the magnitude of political repression, the kind and severity of social adversity, the degree of social crisis, and the likelihood of social demoralization are issues that are concerned with power, or the lack thereof. Along practically every dimension of social stratification, powerful societal forces effectively and intentionally suppress African Americans as a subordinate group and exclude them from full participation in the society. In actuality, the race problem is a dimension of social control that involves a power relationship. It is one of those forces responsible for conformity that is imposed upon individuals by others. Social norms are produced to protect the social interests of the rule creators and those whom they represent. For example, slavery provided a cheap and controllable source of labor for wealthy European Americans, and Africans were an easily accessible pool of labor for this status. Their racial distinction was an obvious identification mark and further served as justification for enslavement. Thus, race became a discriminatory and legal condition for enslavement. After the abolition of slavery, race continued to serve a discriminatory function and a justification for legal segregation; hence, race was used for the maintenance of white superiority. Even today, race is still a factor in separating African Americans from mainstream American life, economically, politically, educationally, and residentially. In short, race that was first used to justify enslavement of Africans for the benefit of wealthy European Americans was later redefined to sustain white race/class hegemony.

Therefore, the treatment of symptoms cannot cure (although it may alleviate) the discomfort. Since the issue is about power, then the race problem is a political class conflict, an observation previously made by sociologist Oliver C. Cox ([1948] 1970), who asserts that the racial struggle has always been a political class struggle: "If there is to be an overthrow of the system, it will be achieved by way of a political-class struggle . . . It will not come by way of an open interracial matching of power. As a matter of fact, the struggle has never been between all black and all white people--it is a political-class struggle" (573). The black power movement of the 1960s tentatively took this direction, rising on the heels of the frustrated civil rights movement, at a time that saw an explosion of urban riots. As explained by journalist Robert Allen (1969),

> [B]lack power emerged initially as an effort to reform the social system. At that time black militants were sophisticated enough to know that integration was not satisfactory because it did not affect the oppression suffered by most blacks. Hence it was logical to conclude that only the political

> integration of black people <u>as a group</u> into American society
> could offer any real hope. Therefore [Stokeley] Carmichael
> defined black power as group integration into the political
> process (49).

Thus, black power as a concept attempted to move the struggle beyond winning legal concessions and in the direction of ascertaining political power. Emphasis was placed on group solidarity, economic cooperatives, black consciousness, revolutionary Black Nationalism, and the international context of African American liberation. It concluded that because the race problem is a political class conflict, it must be overcome by political class struggle.

Political class struggle is a product of societal organization. The political and sociological literature is abundant with distinctions between the rich and the poor, the haves and the have-nots, the powerful and the powerless. As pointed out by political theorist Gaetano Mosca (1939),

> Among the constant facts and tendencies that are to be found
> in all political organisms, one is so obvious that it is apparent
> to the most casual eye. In all societies--from societies that
> are very meagerly developed and have barely attained the
> dawning of civilization, down to the most advanced and
> powerful societies--two classes of people appear--a class that
> rules and a class that is ruled. The first, class, always the
> less numerous, performs all political functions, monopolizes
> power and enjoys the advantages that power brings, whereas
> the second, the more numerous class, is directed and
> controlled by the first, in a manner that is now more or less
> legal, now more or less arbitrary, and violent, and supplies
> the first, in appearance at least, with material means of
> subsistence and with the instrumentalities that are essential
> to the vitality of the political organism (50).

However, all these citations refer to the idea of political class struggle. The political class has its own unique, discernible meaning, purpose, and method.

The political class is not a social class. The political class denotes a group of persons with common interests; it has no relationship of social rank, lineage, income, or occupation (although its membership my come disproportionately from a particular social class). The political class is a power group whose membership crosses social-class lines, is class conscious, and is organized for conflict. As pointed out by Marxist philosopher Georg Lukacs (1971), class-consciousness is "<u>the sense, become conscious, of the historical role of the class</u>" (73). In other words, it is the awareness of a specific group of its self-interest (as opposed to individual interests) in the present historical condition. Sociologist Oliver C. Cox ([1948] 1970) clearly distinguishes political and social classes when he writes,

> Social classes form a system of co-operating conceptual status entities; political classes, on the other hand, do not constitute a system at all, for they are antagonistic. The political class is a power group which tends to be organized for conflict; the social class is never organized, for it is a concept only. Although the political class is ordinarily weighted with persons from a special sector of the social-status gradient, it may include persons from every position. Hence we do not speak of political classes as forming a hierarchy; they may conceivably split the social hierarchy vertically; therefore, there is here no primary conception of social stratification. In other words, members of the political class ordinarily do not have a common social status. These classes, therefore, are not thought of as social-class strata but as organizations arrayed face to face against each other (154-155).

The purpose of a political class is control of the political system. Its fundamental objective is the annihilation of the existing political system and the institution of a new political system, which will serve the interests of the political class in power. Once again, says Cox, "in class-conflict situations the object on trial is not an administration but rather a political system; the whole institutional order may be marked for weeding out" (156).

Hence, the political class uses revolution as a method of displacing the existing government. The political class must have at its disposal the machinery of policy and propaganda, as well as a judicious schema or revolutionary theory for deposing the existing government. At the same time, the political class must reveal why it is distinct from the present society and present a way of life that is both superior to and incompatible with the existing social and political system.

Therefore, the political class is a power group that aims to control the government. Political class conflict is the result of consciousness born of agitation, which requires leadership and organization. Hence, the political class has potential existence until it is provoked into becoming conscious and organized for conflict. And once political class-consciousness is brought to cognizance, the political class must compose an effective revolutionary ideology that reveals its distinction from the existing society; critiques the existing social, economic, and political arrangements; and proposes the ideal substitute.

Only a dominant political class has the power and resources to establish and sustain the institution of slavery, the bipartite system of racial segregation, and the social enforcement of racism. These are benefits that accrue to that group capable of exercising power over other groups and inflicting cruelty upon them. The white, slave-owning elite of colonial America (and later within an independent America) was such a political class: Politically experienced, educated, wealthy, and cosmopolitan, they required an economic, political, and social system that reflected their interests. The economic objective of this class was the control of labor, and slavery was the preferred method; the rationalization was white supremacy. However, the rationalization served a dual purpose: (1) It maintained the dominance of the white ruling class, and (2) it served as a buttress against white lower-class aspirations. Hence, white supremacy and racism would serve as the cornerstone to maintain the class structure. The institution of slavery was driven by a need for labor that was privately owned, denied in perpetuity ownership of the means of production, and denied control over the products of labor. This mode of production was necessary to the white ruling class, which depended on slavery for its wealth and maintenance of its political domination.

In order to sustain the status quo, a rationalization was proffered. As pointed out by sociologist Jack M. Bloom (1987), "Because of the importance of white supremacy in maintaining the class structure, this elite, based on the ownership of land, had a vested interest in perpetuating racism. Southern racism was thus intertwined with the class structure of the South and was, in fact, its lynchpin" (18). Thus, racism maintained the oppressive treatment of persons of African descent, and it duped the white lower class into accepting this rationalization, against their own best interests.

During and following Reconstruction, the aim was to deny African Americans political power, because "without political power, blacks could more easily be forced into economic subservience and become the controlled labor force that the merchant-landlord class felt it needed" (Bloom 1987, 20). However, asserts Bloom, "white supremacy did not mean that all whites were to be supreme" (20). It was simply a "code word" and strategy deceptively used to scare the white, lower class about "Negro domination;" it was a strategy raised any time the merchant-landlord class position was threatened (20).

Through political maneuvering, the Southern white ruling class, via the Democratic Party, was able to undermine Republican Party influence by, among other things, making the Republican Party a party of African Americans trying to establish black domination. The Democratic Party was thus made "the party of all classes of Southern whites" (Bloom 1987, 31).

Additionally, the Southern ruling class used the Ku Klux Klan and other terrorist organizations to control African American labor and poor whites. Protected by the judicial authorities, the Klan and other such organizations received widespread support of the white community. Consequently, "[if] the blacks had no rights, no protection, then they couldn't stand up to the landlord or the poor white" (Bloom 1987, 33).

Election fraud and violence were also used to subvert the Republican Party and African American political participation. Republican votes were either not counted or undercounted; African Americans active in the Republican Party were subjected to economic pressure; and African

Americans were crushed by intimidation, violence, and murder (Bloom 1987, 33). With the end of Reconstruction, "white supremacy now meant that whoever controlled the state government controlled the whole state. And, since only one party was of any significance, whoever controlled it controlled the state, including most local government" (Bloom 1987, 35).

With white supremacy entrenched, the Southern white ruling class set the tone for race relations throughout the nation. For the first half of the twentieth century, African Americans were second-class citizens. Southern, white ruling-class domination was now secure.

But by the time the Depression arrived, the decision was made to industrialize the South and bring it in line with the rest of the American economy. The New Deal of Franklin Roosevelt changed the economic base and character of the South: Manufacturing began to supplant agriculture, urbanization increased, the Southern economy became more diversified, and the rural-agricultural dominance of the Southern governing class became weakened. World War II expanded the New Deal and firmly established the welfare state that undermined the old Southern economic and political order. By the end of World War II, the foundation for a new economy was shifting economic power to the urban centers and profoundly impacting Southern social arrangements (Bloom 1987, 66-68).

Nationally, the base of the Democratic Party was becoming more urban and was enhanced by the movement of voting African Americans in the North to the Democratic Party en masse. The challenge to the old Southern ruling class now came from within the Democratic Party itself. The liberal wing of the Democratic Party began to purge the party of its conservative Southern bloc, and once again race became the pivotal issue. But this time, the old Southern, white ruling class would see its economic and political hegemony come to an end, as it was now being replaced as the "most central class" and in the process losing "its political leadership, as well" (Bloom 1987, 73).

As pointed out by Bloom (1987), this set the tone for the civil rights movement. The old Southern white ruling class had used segregation "to defend its own power and position" (214). The civil rights movement, with the assistance of the federal government, succeeded in defeating this class, something the first Reconstruction failed to do. As a result of new economic circumstances, the old Southern elite was diminished in significance and "new classes--the business and middle classes--emerged, with different needs and interests" (215). Consequently, these new classes found it to be in their economic and political interests to "intervene to counter the resistance to civil rights demands and to accommodate blacks" (215). The shift in economic conditions could now be accompanied by a redistribution of political power as a result of the civil rights movement.

But as the civil rights movement shifted its focus, according to Bloom (1987), from desegregation to concentration on African Americans' social class position, the civil rights coalition disintegrated. What had brought the disparate forces of white business and African American civil rights interests together had been achieved. They had united against the old regime, and "a new regime [was] brought into being" (218). Political class power was reshuffled, and the new issue of changes to the class system was now troubling to middle-class, white America. The new political class had resolved itself to combat segregation and overt racial discrimination, but challenges to the class structure did not benefit business and the urban economy in general (219).

So the federal government's participation in the civil rights movement, along with that of the new class of Southern white business, was not what it had initially appeared to be. Although the status of African Americans changed, it was also obvious that actual conditions were incompatible with the promises of civil rights laws and egalitarian public policies. And when actual experience was compared to the promises, the political response to the civil rights movement amounted to a gesture of symbolic reassurance, that is, a substitute measure implemented to dispel threat or emotional tension. This observation was made early on by social scientists Harrell Rogers and Charles Bullock (1972), who make the point that the government's commitment to civil rights was weak and disproportionate:

> There should be no mistake that if the government wants compliance with its civil rights policy it can achieve it-- possibly not immediately but certainly through persistent efforts.
>
> The national government's commitment to gaining compliance with civil rights laws had typically been neither strong nor consistent. It has normally moved into areas of civil rights gingerly, even timidly. Early efforts, which are usually symbolic, recognize certain rights, develop limited machinery for enforcement, and provided rather weak penalties for noncompliance . . . (194-195).

Political scientist Murray Edelman (1971) complements this position in his observation that

> The enactment of civil rights laws and the proclamation of egalitarian public policies are symbols that they [African Americans] can expect equal treatment and that policy makers view them as deserving equal treatment . . .
>
> Some public policies therefore create for blacks a belief in their right to equal treatment, while at the same time daily experiences and other governmental actions signal the absence of progress toward that goal (19-20).

Therefore, the effects of the civil rights movement have left many African Americans relatively untouched by change, leaving in its wake only feelings of cynicism, resignation, and futility. None of what the government actually did was capable of significantly altering the position of African Americans. In the final analysis, the government's response produced an image of change greater than the change that has actually occurred. In fact, what has occurred is not integration, but adaptation. True integration on the social level involves unifying people into a harmonious whole, while maintaining the capacity of each individual to make choices and participate in the historical and cultural process. But the civil rights movement was unable to break through to the point where African Americans could freely choose; instead, they remained subjected to the choices of others and consequently were forced to adapt and adjust. They were diminished to spectators and offered "assistencialism," a term used by Brazilian educator Paulo Freire (1973) "to describe policies of financial or social assistance which attacks symptoms, but not causes, of social ills" (15), that effectively closed off their participation in the historical process, treated them as passive objects, and shut down dialogue.

However, from the general white American perspective this is not the case. Since the Democratic Party was responsible for bringing the federal government into the civil rights movement, large segments of the Democratic white electorate have progressively grown disenchanted with their party. And, according to political scientists Robert Huckfeldt and Carol W. Kohfeld (1989), this "white disenchantment with the Democratic party is fundamentally rooted in the politics of race," because white voters "are ill at ease with a party that is fundamentally dependent upon, as well as responsive to, the American black electorate" (39). As the white electorate perceived the Democratic Party as favorable to African American interests, they became disenchanted with the push for African American equal rights. The Republican Party stepped in at this point and began to establish itself as favorable to the white electorate, which further "widened the breach between the national Democratic party and white southern Democrats" (11). Consequently, thanks to political realignment within the South, the Democratic Party is now seen as the party of African Americans. This racial shift in party support is fundamentally rooted in the politics of race. What this does is prohibit a class-based coalition among African Americans and whites.

Thus, race continues to serve as a wedge that disguises the class nature of American political arrangements. It continues as the lynchpin that serves white political-class domination. As pointed out by Huckfeldt and Kohfeld (1989), "Working-class and lower-middle-class whites are frequently unwilling to participate in a coalition that depends upon the votes of blacks in order to win elections" (ix). This potential coalition is disrupted by the politics of race, because "as long as the majority of blacks belong to a disadvantaged class, the social and political isolation of blacks benefits advantaged groups in American politics" (1-2) and disrupts politics along class lines. Today, as during Reconstruction, white political hegemony depends on the clever manipulation of race to hold class at bay; however, today this is not limited to the South but spans the nation as a whole.

So, race was and still is the critical link in white, ruling-class domination. Time and time again, race has been used to avert social change that threatened the ruling class. Consequently, racism has been the most potent ingredient in white, ruling-class hegemony and has served as a buttress for the status quo social, economic, and political structures.

Hence, since the very beginning of the nation's history, there has been a very powerful and well-organized political class that has not been challenged to any significant degree by organized forces within the nation. It can be said that there exists within the United States today no other competitive political class. Although there are two dominant political parties in the United States, there is only one political class: that of the white, wealthy, upper class. The Democratic and Republican parties are two factions representing the same fundamental interests; they are subdivisions of the one political class. As pointed out by political scientist Michael Parenti (1995),

> [A]lmost all the social institutions existing in this [American] society, along with the immense material and vocational resources they possess, are under plutocratic control, ruled by nonelected, self-selected, self-perpetuating groups of affluent corporate representatives who are answerable to no one but themselves. These institutions shape many of our everyday experiences and much of our social consciousness; yet we have no vote, no portion of ownership, and legal decision-making power within them. The power they exercise over us is hierarchical and nondemocratic (34).

Sociologist G. William Domhoff (1978) refers to this political class as a "power elite," that is, "the leadership group or operating arm of the ruling class" (13). It is this "power elite," and not the entire membership of this class, that is involved in ruling. In fact, as pointed out by Domhoff, "[T]here always have been carefully groomed and carefully selected employees from lower social classes whose advancement to important positions has been dependent upon their ability to solve problems and attain goals that are determined by the needs and desires of the ruling class" (15). Taken as a whole, this "plutocracy" or "power elite" composes what political scientist Bertram Gross (1980) calls the "American Establishment," which he defines as "a complex of complexes, a far-flung network of power centers . . . held together . . . by mutual interests, shared ideologies, and accepted procedures for mediating their endless conflicts" (55). It is a blending of "polity and economy," a marriage "of big business and big government" (55).

This political class extends back to the nation's founding, when a political class representing the nation's intellectual and economic elite put the United States together. This political class has sustained itself by "the movement of talented and ambitious individuals from the lower strata" into its ranks, hence "providing for a slow and continuous modification of the ruling classes," while maintaining its domination and avoiding revolution (Dye and Zeigler 2000, 59).

Although the race problem is a political-class issue, African Americans are not an organized power group unified by class-consciousness. In general, African Americans have no intention of annihilating the existing political system; they have no revolutionary ideology or substitute for the present social, economic, and political arrangements; and they are politically unorganized and lack class-consciousness.

The intentions of African Americans have never been total destruction of the American social, economic, and political system. Although there have been groups and individuals within the African American population who have advocated radical ideologies, their ideologies did not propose the overthrow of the American political system. African Americans have generally, since the antebellum period, been socially driven toward full and equal participation in American society. Their desire has been acceptance by whites and unconditional recognition as Americans. They continually address themselves to the limitations on their participation in American society, while wishing to participate in the American social milieu and enjoy the social advantages accorded whites. On this point alone, African Americans fail to fulfill the requirements of a political class. With the exception of certain separatist tendencies within African American social and political thought, African Americans in general have striven toward integration and assimilation with the mainstream American society. And it is toward white opposition to this aspiration, not the fundamental structure of the socio-economic and political system, that African Americans have continually addressed themselves.

African Americans as a whole also have no revolutionary ideology. Because they have been socially driven toward full and equal participation, African Americans have never felt the intellectual push to develop such an ideology. With the exception of groups and individuals within the African American population who have adopted alternative ideologies (such as Black Nationalism, socialism, or communism), there is no evidence of a uniquely African-American revolutionary ideology. Since African Americans in general have sought not to overthrow the system but to instead become equal participants within it, their struggles have been more reformist than revolutionary in nature. Consequently, African Americans have not distinguished themselves as an oppositional political class.

Also, African Americans as a collective are not politically organized. There are a multiplicity of African American organizations with different programs and objectives. These organizations have a significant constituency simultaneously operative on many social, economic, and political issues affecting African Americans. However, these organizations display very little, if any, cooperation and coordination toward political goals; such would require comprehensive class organization that presupposes the formation of class-consciousness. Instead, African Americans have found it expedient to cast their lot with one or another of the major political parties.

But most significantly, what inhibits African Americans from constituting a political class is a lack of class-consciousness. Instead, African Americans are unified by race- consciousness--a totally different phenomenon. Race-consciousness is universal and is a product of the racial situation. It refers to race relations among distinct peoples (Cox [1948] 1970, 428-430). On the other hand, class-consciousness is particular and is a product of the political situation. The race-conscious group is aware only in terms of its sentimental interests, but the political class is aware of the nature and interests of the group. Therefore, a race-conscious group may be divided on the basis of social, economic, and political interests, but the political class is unified on these interests. Thus, class-consciousness is a much more cohesive element than race-consciousness and is the catalyst for developing a political class. Hence, African Americans comprise an objective, empirically-existing class connected by race but conflicted by the particular interests of individuals for their own social advancement that is contrary to the interests of the class as a whole. Thus, status-consciousness prevents and masks the emergence of class-consciousness. Since there is no identity of interests of the class as a whole (with the exception of racial discrimination), there is no basis for the rise of a comprehensive class organization, that is, a political organization capable of enforcing its own class interests. Consequently, with no identity of interests and no political organization, there is no subjective awareness; there is no class-consciousness.

Many factors have interacted to thwart the development of political class-consciousness among African Americans. As previously mentioned, lowly status, social adversity, social crisis, and social demoralization have acted to restrain the development of political class-consciousness. The very structure of African-American thought has been shaped by their existential condition. The energies and resources of African Americans have been deflected away from courses potentially more rewarding and toward either more traditional courses of action with little political pay-off or the evolution of an oppositional culture mired in pathology, a manifestation of social demoralization.

This failure can partly be attributed to African American leadership. Instead of encouraging reflection and action to disrupt the political system, African American leaders have, by and large, opted for electioneering and lobbying as a means of integration with the larger American society. In a rather caustic critique of African American leadership, sociologist Oliver C. Cox ([1948] 1970) asserts that African American leaders must perform the delicate task of "antagonistic-co-operation" (572) under the baffling circumstance of being "a friend of the enemy" (572-573). Such a stance, according to Cox, requires that African American leaders advocate for the African American cause, but with a modicum of aggression and militancy that would incur white resentment. Hence, such leaders understand the tacit agreement that their leadership is dependent upon white acceptance and toleration. Writes Cox, "No contemporary Negro leader of major significance, then, can be totally void of at least a modicum of the spirit of 'Uncle Tom;' ingratiation, compromise, and appeasement must be his specialties" (573). For Cox, the solution is political class struggle with African Americans in alliance with white democratic forces, but African American leadership is weakest at this point.

Social critic Harold Cruse (1967, 1968) has also argued along these lines, demonstrating in historical detail the crisis of African American leadership that has resulted in shifts, failures, and lost opportunities for African Americans. Originally, Cruse put forward a theory of black culturalism as a philosophy and methodology for radical politics and the achievement of African American liberation. Later, Cruse (1987), in an exceptional historical analysis of contemporary African American politics, asserts the only option remaining for African American leadership is cultural pluralism under which African Americans must form a political party that must systematically reorganize "many areas of black life into, first a <u>political bloc,</u> then cultural blocs, and then into whatever internal economic organizations are possible within a capitalistic, free-market system" (378).

Although Cruse's thesis moves in the direction of political class-consciousness and political class struggle among African Americans, the cultural pluralist nature of the argument presupposes an acceptance of the current American political and economic system and of working within it. And again, this is not real political class struggle.

Psychologist Kenneth B. Clark (1965) also makes reference to the weakness of African American political leadership when he asserts that African American political leadership is severely inexperienced and politically unsophisticated:

> Because their house of political power is built on sand without a solid base of economic or social influence, ghetto politicians are likely to accept a limited jurisdiction and to seek immediate and concrete rewards. They often subject themselves to the control of others they believe to hold primary power, and some are prepared to make petty deals and to toy with political corruption. But even in corruption the Negro is accorded second-class citizenship . . . In political patronage, too, Negro politicians are restricted to the lower levels of reward. The hard facts generally tend to limit the outreach and the effectiveness of the ghetto politicians. Unable to compete successfully for power or patronage, they tend to compete among themselves for the available crumbs; and this struggle, in turn, makes them more vulnerable to manipulation by real political leadership—i.e., white leadership. When no one has much patronage or much power, rivalry for a minimal share keeps everyone divided and everyone impotent (156).

Finally, philosopher and theologian Cornel West (1993) weighs in on the topic, asserting that the crisis in African American leadership is the result of the "deterioration of personal, familial, and communal relations among African Americans" (56); consequently, the development of a collective and critical consciousness suffers. Also, the post-civil rights era has witnessed, among specifically African American political leaders, "the relative lack of authentic anger and the relative absence of genuine humility" (58) necessary for bold and defiant leadership. And, says West, African American intellectual leaders "tend to be mere academicians, narrowly confined to specialized disciplines with little sense of the broader life of the mind and hardly any engagement with battles in the streets" (62).

Another significant factor that hampers the development of political class-consciousness is the increased economic polarization among African Americans (that is, a worsening African American lower-class and an increasing middle-class of affluent African Americans), and hence class stratification, brought on by the civil rights gains of the 1960s. Contingent with this development was a rightward shift in American politics that was partly a response to the turmoil of the 1960s and partly a response to the perceived failures and excesses of liberalism that fostered welfare dependency, sapped personal initiative, contributed to an ethic of irresponsibility, created an unjustified sense of entitlement among the poor and racial minorities, and accommodated the breakdown in social behavior (Rueter, 1995). This newfound conservatism was prevalent not only among white ethnics, but also among a growing number of African Americans who were given considerable attention by the Reagan administration and the Republican Party. These African-American neoconservatives act as bulwarks for the status quo by downplaying race and making opposition to affirmative action and liberal social welfare programs acceptable. Also, by minimizing race, African American conservatives imply that African American disadvantages are due not to racial discrimination, but deficiencies in African American cultural, family, social organization, and psychological make up. This kind of thinking undoubtedly motivates white Republicans and white conservatives, because it further compromises the ideological divisions in African American politics and threatens the political hegemony of liberalism among African Americans. However, as pointed out by political scientist Theodore Rueter (1995), "Republicans do not want too many blacks in the GOP, given that this would make it difficult for them to exploit the racial issue in American politics" (101).

Therefore, the only viable option for African Americans is real political class struggle. The race problem is an issue of power, and, as an issue of power, the race problem is a political class conflict. Consequently, the entire political system must be challenged with a revolutionary ideology that exposes the nature, intent, and privilege of the dominant political class. Additionally, the new revolutionary ideology must convert African American race-consciousness into class-consciousness, through which African Americans can confront the American power structure from the position of a contending political class. This is the only way that African Americans can critically recognize the true cause of their subordinate position and, through class-consciousness, act in their class interests.

CHAPTER FOUR

From Revolutionary Potential to Revolution

Any type of social stratification that splits the social gradient hierarchically devalues and dehumanizes those beneath the top in varying degrees. Since African Americans tend to be always at or near the bottom of the status gradient, they are the least valued in society. But the ascribed status given African Americans is predicated on a wrong. Consequently, this wrong has engendered, among African Americans, tremendous revolutionary potential. However, the revolution must be not only socially transformative but also therapeutic.

As noted previously in Hegelian terms, the African slave was reduced to the status of a non-human thing. As a thing, the slave had no rights and was subject to the will of the slave-master. The slave-master, therefore, appropriated the slave as a means to his or her own individual interests and satisfactions. However, this is an absurdity. To reduce a person to the status of a thing is a contradiction: The slave cannot simultaneously be a non-person thing and a person. But this was James Madison's absurd reasoning in his defense of the three-fifths compromise, which characterized the African slave as both person and property. Hence, slavery was a negation of the slave's rights as a person. It was the exploitation and injury of persons as a means to another's ends. This is wrong, because the situation of slavery is in opposition to the principle of rightness, which dictates that a person should not be a means to another's ends. To effectively remove a person from the category of human is to deny that he deserves recognition as a person or deserves human rights. This emphatically breaks the bounds of what is right and just. As observed by philosopher Arthur Schopenhauer (1962),

> A hundred records, old and new, produce the conviction that in his unrelenting cruelty man is in no way inferior to the tiger and the hyaena. A forcible example is supplied by a publication of the year 1844 entitled <u>Slavery and the International Slave Trade in the United States of North America: being replies to questions transmitted by the British Anti-slavery Society to the American Anti-slavery Society</u>. This book constitutes one of the heaviest indictments against the human race. No one can put it down without a feeling of horror, and few without tears. For whatever the reader may have ever heard, or imagined, or dreamt, of the unhappy condition of slavery, or indeed of human cruelty in general, it will seem small to him when he reads of the way in which those devils in human form, those bigoted, church-going, strictly Sabbatarian rascals--and in particular the Anglican priests among them--treated their innocent black brothers, who by wrong and violence had got into their diabolical clutches (283-284).

And the wrong did not end when slavery ended; it continued under a bipartite racial system. When the bipartite racial system was legally ended, de facto segregation and racial prejudice continued as social practice.

Having possessed and used the slave, American society then relinquished the slave through emancipation. But emancipation was not so much a negation of the wrongs of slavery as it was a denial to the slave owner of his particular property, the slave.

So the contradiction remained in the presumption of rightness. The denial of African Americans' humanity established a relationship of oppression that rejected the universal content of right. Hence, right is on the side of those African Americans whose response to oppression is based on the desire to pursue the right to be human. And the pursuit of right is the only way to resolve the contradiction. African Americans accomplish this through their struggle for right, in which they "take away the oppressors' power to dominate and suppress and restore to the oppressors the humanity they had lost in the exercise of oppression" (Freire 1970, 42).

Consequently, emancipation was a fraud, a disguise. It deceived African Americans into believing they would get their rights, but the supposed right of emancipation and citizenship was an illusion. The fraud was then aided by coercion that deprived African Americans their due. This was another degree of wrong supported by an absurd act of projection, interpreted by Brazilian educator Paulo Freire (1970):

> Violence is initiated by those who oppress, who exploit, who fail to recognize others as persons--not by those who are oppressed, exploited, and unrecognized. It is not the

unloved who initiate disaffection, but those who cannot love because they love only themselves. It is not the helpless, subject to terror, who initiate terror, but the violent, who with their power create the concrete situation which begets the "rejects of life." It is not the tyrannized who initiate despotism, but the tyrants. It is not the despised who initiate hatred, but those who despise. It is not those whose humanity is denied them who negate man, but those who denied that humanity (thus negating their own as well). Force is used not by those who have become weak under the preponderance of the strong, but by the strong who have emasculated them (41).

The act of fraud aided by coercion was a crime. It effectively denied that African Americans (the victims of this crime) had any rights. It infringed upon the freedoms and rights of African Americans, and it annulled the expression or determinate existence of African Americans as persons. But unlike fraud, the act of crime comes about in defiance of the victim's thinking. The crime was a conscious, purposive act in which the victims suffered injury. In the case of African Americans, the injury is stolen labor power and social opportunities, as well as the infliction of cruelty, brutality, inhumanity, and de jure and de facto racial discrimination.

The negation of wrong in the form of fraud and crime is correctable through compensation for the wrong in the form of reparation. Randall Robinson, founder of TransAfrica, provides interesting examples of ignored proposals for restitution to African Americans in his book, The Debt: What America Owes to Blacks (2000). According to Robinson the first instance came when President "Andrew Johnson vetoed legislation that would have provided compensation to ex-slaves" (204). Then, Cornelius Jones in 1915 "filed a lawsuit against the United States Department of the Treasury in an attempt to recover sixty-eight million dollars for former slaves," (206) which was appropriated through a federal tax on cotton produced by slave labor, but the case was dismissed by a federal appeals court. Later, Robinson writes, came the publication of Yale Law School professor Boris Bittker's book, The Case for Black Reparations, "which made the argument that slavery, Jim Crow, and a general climate of race-based discrimination in America had combined to do grievous social and economic injury to African Americans" (202). The book, which argued that some program for reparations was necessary, was generally ignored. In April of 1993, the Organization of African Unity drafted a declaration "against the United States and the countries of western Europe for restitution," (218) which also went ignored. Finally, Robinson cites Jamaican human rights lawyer Dudley Thompson, who argues that there are legal precedents for reparations in international law. According to Thompson,

Not only is there a moral debt but there is clearly established precedence in law based on the principle of unjust enrichment. In law if a party unlawfully enriches himself by wrongful acts against another, then the party so wronged is entitled to recompense. There have been some 15 cases in which the highest tribunals including the International Court at the Hague have awarded large sums as reparations based on this law (221).

However, the negation of wrong, and hence crime, is punishment. And punishment must negate the wrong not in the shallow sense of deterrence, reform, retribution, revenge, or vendetta, but rather in the sense of correction that is rehabilitative. Thus, punishment is an act of justice, and justice requires reckoning. However, it is not reckoning in the absurd sense of an eye for an eye or a tooth for a tooth, but reckoning in the rational sense of restoring, strengthening, and confirming what is right. And since it is the state, the political apparatus, which has legitimized and legalized this wrong--slavery, fraud, and crime against African Americans--through acts of violence, it is the state which must be punished. Having asserted violence as its law, then the application of this law to itself is justice, because the measure of its punishment must be derived from its own actions--that is, violence. In other words, punishment is the form of the crime turned round against the perpetrator.

Consequently, the government must be overthrown. Because supplanting one class with another requires overthrowing the government, and because the political class in power controls the decisive instruments of violence, political-class struggle is violent. Only by relieving the political class in power of its control over the instruments of violence, and hence the government, can revolution be successful. Anything less is simply reform, as pointed out by Rosa Luxemburg, revolutionary Marxist and a martyr of the revolutionary struggle in Germany during World War I. Concerning class struggle, she writes,

> [P]eople who pronounce themselves in favor of the method of legislative reform in place of and in contradistinction to the conquest of political power, a social revolution, do not really choose a more tranquil, calmer and slower road to the same goal, but a different goal. Instead of taking a stand for the establishment of a new society, they take a stand for surface modifications of the old society (Cox [1948] 1970, 170).

Violence, then, is a necessary consequence of political class struggle. The political class in power will never yield without violence; it will not be argued or reasoned out of its position. According to sociologist Robert Michels, "Attempts at persuasion fail miserably when they are addressed to the privileged classes, in order to induce these to abandon, to their own disadvantage, as a class and as individuals, the leading positions they occupy in society" (Cox [1948] 1970, 163). Clearly this is an enormous presumption to expect the political class in power to commit class suicide for the asking. As Michels says, "[a] class considered as a whole never spontaneously surrenders its position of advantage. It never recognizes any moral reason sufficiently powerful to compel it to abdicate in favor of its 'poorer brethren.' Such action is prevented, if by nothing else, by class egoism" (Cox [1948] 1970, 163-164). Along these same lines theologian James H. Cone ([1970] 1990), commenting on the work of Reinhold Niebuhr, observes,

> [T]hose in power will never admit that society rewards them far out of proportion to the services they render; and this attitude inevitably makes them enslave all who question their interests. Appeals to reason and religion do not change the balance of power, because both are used to defend the interests of oppressors. Change will take place, according to Niebuhr, when the enslaved recognize that power must be met with power (98).

Having said this, it must be added that no political system, however flexible, is open to fundamental change by legal means. The law, says sociologist Oliver C. Cox ([1948] 1970), "is the instrument of the ruling class; hence it is a logical impossibility for another class to assume power legally" (164). The law fortifies the existing order; it is not some abstraction that can be separated from the political foundation on which it is based or from the political interests that it serves. Therefore, laws are a primary means of repression, which operate under the cover of legitimacy. And laws have been used to restrict African Americans since their arrival on the continent. Consequently, the U.S. Constitution has brought African Americans as far as they can go under its various interpretations. The Bill of Rights, the Fourteenth Amendment, the Fifteenth Amendment, the various acts of Congress, and their judicial reinforcements have proven insufficient guarantees for economic, political, and social equality of African Americans. And as a result, the contemporary relevance of the U.S. Constitution comes into question. The U.S. Constitution was never conceived, written, amended, or interpreted to resolve America's race problem.

Any threat to the reign of a political class is met with intolerance. The threat is often described as treasonous, un-American, ungodly, and adverse to law and order. As observed by political scientist Harold F. Laski, "[W]henever privilege is in danger, it flies into that panic which is the mortal enemy of reason; and it is a waste of time to ask its consideration of arguments that, in another mental climate, it is capable of understanding" (Cox [1948] 1970, 168). Cone ([1970 1990) also remarks on this point that,

> [t]o   assert   one's   freedom   always   involves

encountering the economic and social structures of oppression. When rulers first perceive dissent--a threat to "their" society--their initial response is to try to silence the dissenters by cutting off the sources of physical existence and social involvement. This is to remind the rebels who is boss. Oppressors hope that by making it difficult to live, rebels will come around to seeing the world as oppressors see it.

Coupled with economic oppression is social ostracism. The intention is to demonstrate the perversity of rebel involvement by picturing them as destroyers of "the good." At no time are the rebels given the opportunity to define their way of looking at the world . . . (97-98).

However, as pointed out by Cox ([1948] 1970), cooperation is not the aim. Law and order is to the advantage of the dominant political class; conciliatory discussion and negotiation acknowledges the dominant political class' prestige. The vanquishing of the old leaders and the old system is the end of the attacking class, and this is "a problem which the ruling class cannot be expected to discuss" (168). Consequently, compromise and appeasement cannot settle the basic antagonism, because political class antagonism is irreconcilable. And "the sanctimonious abhorrence displayed by the ruling class and its apologists against the use of violence in the class struggle is rooted in the desire to maintain the integrity of its class monopoly of violence" (168-169).

Therefore, it may be surmised that African Americans have the most potent and justifiable revolutionary capabilities of any group in America. The gap between African American expectations and gratifications has always been wide, leading to intense frustration and hostility. Although the frustration has been, in general, contained within the political system and has often been modified, it has never been displaced. It is thus this long, persistent denial of fulfillment and atonement that is of revolutionary potential. Despite their lowly status, social adversity, social crisis, and social demoralization, African Americans have continued to assert their worth and have attempted to validate their claim to human rights. Theirs is a history of protest against enslavement, subordination, cruelty, and inhumanity that began with their seizure in Africa. The African American has used many methods to protest: slave revolts, petitions, appeals, court suits, sabotage, passive resistance, and riots. Yet, on the whole, African Americans remain outside of, and alienated from, much of American life. Hence, African American social movements, from slavery to the present, "contain the seeds of a future political revolution," although these social movements have not given "rise to an immediate restructuring of the state apparatus and the basic power relations within" American society (Marable 1985, 72). African American social movements have yet to make the existing state apparatus a target for fundamental change, nor created the conditions necessary for the ruling class to be unable to live in the old way.

Nevertheless, African American social movements as "pre-revolutionary modes of social class struggle" have set the historical stage for revolution (Marable 1985, 72-73).

Therefore, what endows African Americans with the most potent revolutionary capabilities is the historical fact that they are in the vanguard of fundamental social change in American society. The logical conclusion is that there is an uneven development of political activity and an uneven development of political consciousness between African Americans and white Americans. African Americans are much more keenly aware of their limited capacity to influence the political system, and they are much less trusting of political leaders. This is a result of the political realities that have continuously deprived African Americans of political power (Abramson 1983, 160-164, 219-223). As a consequence of the racial dimension of their struggle, the African American struggle for political justice is far less fragmented, and their view of political reality more correct as a result. Also, African American leadership has been constant in its attempt to intervene in society in a permanent and continuous way, however modest and limited that constitutes the basis for the justification that they are a vanguard group.

The African American situation is unique because it stems from a racial component. The un-American experience of the African American is a purely racial experience. It reflects a dualism, a dichotomous absurdity in which the African American both is and is not an American, is and is not a citizen, is related and is unrelated to the nation. Consequently, the African American response has also reflected a dichotomous absurdity of wanting out and wanting in. The appeal of "wanting out" is evidenced in the tragedy of suicide to escape bondage, emigration, separatism, and isolation. However, there has been simultaneously the desire of "wanting in," in which the struggle conceded to working within the system and by its rules, adopting mainstream goals, methods, and values in the attempt to be included in the mainstream of American politics and economics.

As a result of the African American revolutionary capabilities and their unique situation, the African American is in the existential position of what philosopher Albert Camus (1956) describes as metaphysical rebellion, "the movement by which man protests against his condition" (23). It is a movement that rejects and refuses to acknowledge "the power that compels [one] to live in this condition" of suffering, death, and incompleteness (24). But metaphysical rebellion is also an affirmation, a conviction that there are limits, that there are rights, and that there is a boundary beyond which the infringement and intrusion on the rights of others will not be tolerated.

The very condition of social demoralization is a state of metaphysical rebellion. From the very beginning, the African in America disapproved of the condition of slavery. From this, a history unfolded of calling into question a power that asserts superiority and inflicts suffering individually and collectively. It is a stage in which toleration has reached its limit.

But where do African Americans go from here? What other avenues are open to a demoralized people? Since the demise of the civil rights movement, it remains abundantly clear that African Americans will not be fully integrated into American society any time soon, and since the prospect of social revolution is in the distant future, it has been necessary for African Americans to at least think about transitional programs aimed at community development and the facilitation of class-consciousness.

During the late 1960s, "Black Power" advocates called for cooperative economic ventures within the African American community. As asserted by Stokely Carmichael, cooperative economics means it is necessary that "black money go into black pockets . . .We want to see money go back into the community and used to benefit it. We want to see the cooperative concept applied in business and banking" (Allen 1969, 52). This idea was more or less a modification of W.E. B. DuBois' "cooperative commonwealth." DuBois called for a planned economy within African American communities that would insure adequate income to the community, establish unionism, eliminate private profit, provide socialized health-care, organize African American professionals to provide the needed services, and establish African American control of educational systems. DuBois' vision was of a planned, self-sufficient economy within the African American community that would facilitate community development, socialize property relations, strengthen family and group ties, and foster a community dedicated to group advancement (Allen 1969, 274-277).

Around this same time, "Black capitalism" was put forward as a program for solving the race problem. In general, the idea was to create a class of African American capitalists who would demonstrate to African American dissidents that assimilation is possible. The idea was proposed not by African Americans, but by President Richard Nixon and automotive magnate Henry Ford II, as well as business leaders who wished to curb social unrest within the African American community. Roy Innis and Floyd McKissick of the Congress of Racial Equality and economist Robert S. Browne enthusiastically adopted and promoted it (Blair 1977, 164-168). According to journalist Robert Allen (1969), this "black capitalist class would serve thereby as a means of social control by disseminating the ideology and values of the dominant white society throughout the alienated ghetto masses" (212). The idea has generally been criticized as tokenism, in which some elements of the "black bourgeoisie" loyal to the government and corporate America would be placed in prominent positions within government and corporate America as evidence of equal opportunity and as a means of deterring African American social unrest (Baran and Sweezy 1966, 272-273).

Another idea put forward about this same time was reparations, a one-time payment to African Americans for uncompensated slave labor and discrimination. James Forman, one-time executive director of the Student Nonviolent Coordinating Committee, put this forward in his "Black Manifesto." Forman's case for reparations critiques "black capitalism" and demands $500 million from churches and synagogues, to be used for African American economic development along socialist lines. If ignored, sabotage and armed rebellion are threatened (Blair 1977, 169-171). More recently, TransAfrica founder Randall Robinson, in his book The Debt (2000), lays out the framework for a discussion of reparations "with and among those who should feel some moral obligation to atone for slavery and what followed it, along with a commitment to close the social and economic gap between the races, opened and maintained by some 350 years of American racialist policies" (246).

The establishment of an independent African American political party has also been proposed. Such a party would provide the necessary leadership not just for campaigning and garnering votes, but also as a governing tool to extract needed reforms through legal action, electoral politics, and direct action for the explicit purpose of attaining African American self-determination. According to social critic Harold Cruse (1987), such a party must reorganize African American life politically, economically, culturally, educationally, and institutionally. To do so, it must bypass the traditional civil rights leadership, which has been loyal to a Democratic Party that is "no longer capable of accommodating black social priorities, present or future" (379).

Socialist and Marxist theories, which have been the most prevalent and influential revolutionary theories within the American context, have attempted to incorporate the African American experience. As far back as the first quarter of the nineteenth century, African Americans have been aware of, affiliated with, and participated in socialist organizations or socialist-influenced organizations. However, African Americans have encountered many tensions and problems in these organizations.

For example, the "utopian socialists" of the early nineteenth century, though opposed to slavery on moral and economic grounds, found persons of African descent repugnant, as evidenced by their exclusion from membership in utopian communities. Frances Wright's Nashoba community, established in Tennessee in 1825 for persons of African descent, was paternalistically guided by whites who assumed the inferiority of African people required that they be trained and prepared for life outside of slavery. Even upon completion of this training and preparation, African people would not be admitted into American society, because it was assumed that they were incapable of adjusting to Western civilization and would therefore do better among their own people. Furthermore, persons of African descent occupied an inferior status and performed the most menial and laborious work in the Nashoba community. Overall, Nashoba was of little, if any, relevance to persons of African descent. Nashoba's analysis of the African American experience and of slavery in general was deficient in terms of depth and understanding, and it thoroughly lacked any sensitivity or attention to persons of African descent needs, wants, or thoughts (Foner 1977; Pease and Pease 1963).

As for the Marxist or "scientific socialist" organizations, the atmosphere was no better. These organizations also neglected the unique situation of African Americans and had no special policy, interest, or initiative that revolved around African American concerns. Thus, African American interests were subordinated to white, working-class interests.

The strategy used by Marxist socialists was to struggle against slavery so as to free labor. However, following the Civil War these organizations saw the problems of African Americans as no different from those of proletarians in general. Thus, during this period Marxism was unable to interpret the development of different relationships to the economic and political order in terms of race. It ignored the distinct and divided interests racial groups would have to this order. Therefore, the socialist analysis of race relations was unsophisticated in its understanding of the divisions between class and race; as such, it reduced race to class. This limited perspective on race was not very accommodating to African Americans, and individuals would eventually pass through such organizations frustrated by a lack of attention and initiative on the part of socialists (Foner 1977).

Finally, labor organizations, though influenced by socialists, were outright exclusionary and racist. They openly advocated racially-separate unionism and blocked African Americans from jobs, apprenticeships, and trades. Even when African American unions were admitted as affiliates to the national labor unions, racism was tolerated within the national organizations. Furthermore, national labor organizations admitted African Americans only under the politically-opportunist condition that by accepting African Americans into national unions, they would undercut employers' use of African American labor as strikebreakers. Thus, African American labor was used for the political advantages of white labor in their battles with employers. Consequently, African Americans became frustrated by labor unions, which manipulated their loyalty and stood in the way of African American economic advancement (Foner 1977).

Sally Miller (1971), who analyzed the Socialist Party's perspective on African Americans from its founding in 1901 to 1921, provides additional criticisms of the failures of socialist and communist organizations to understand the African American experience in America and to seriously confront the racism and paternalism within their own ranks. Miller writes,

> [T]he Socialist Party in the Progressive Era failed, as did the country at large, to view the Negro as an individual, as a distinct human being in a unique dilemma. The Socialist, concerned as he might be with the downtrodden, the impoverished, the underrepresented, nevertheless did not see the Negro . . . it doubted Negro equality and undertook no meaningful struggles against second-class citizenship (221).

Robert L. Allen (1974), who does a historical investigation of reform movements in the United States, explains that American socialists tended "to dismiss or over-simplify the role of racial antagonism in U.S.

society," and because they lacked "ideological clarity about racism, the socialist parties generally related to black people in an opportunistic and dogmatic manner, resulting in much conflict and bitterness on both sides" (208). And both Harold Cruse (1967) and Ronald Walters (1977), in their critiques of Marxism's relationship to African American struggle, comment on socialist and communist organizations' disconnection from the African American condition and experience. Brunetta Wolfman (1977), in her assessment of the Communist Party's inability to attract the African American masses and maintain African American intellectuals within its ranks, posits several factors, among them a misunderstanding of African American life and thought, its "attacks on the basic institutions, cultural forms, and social structure" within the African American community, and its method of operation which subjected African American intellectuals "to the rigid discipline of the Party and the mechanical assumptions of the Communist faith" (110). Finally, political scientist Mark Naison (1983), in his history of the Communist Party's role in Harlem, points out that "white chauvanism" was prevalent in the party. He makes reference to the party directives against white racial practices, incidents of racial hostility, and resolutions to combat racism within the party.

In the late 1960s, Harold Cruse (1968), in a shift away from traditional protest politics and Marxist politics, proposed that the African American civil rights movement and black power movement could become revolutionary within the American context if it projected "the concept of Cultural Revolution in America" (111). According to Cruse,

> [W]e [African Americans] must locate the weakest sector of the American capitalist "free enterprise" front and strike there. Where is that weak front in the free-enterprise armor? It is in the cultural front. Or better, it is that part of the American economic system that has to do with the ownership and administration of cultural communication in America, i.e., film, theater, radio and television, music, performing and publishing, popular entertainment booking, management, etc. In short, it is that part of the system devoted to the economics and aesthetic ideology involved in the cultural arts of America (110-111).

For Cruse, the African American revolution must go beyond the traditions of liberalism, which has failed to deal adequately with the realities of race in America, and introduce new ideas of social revolution into the bloodstream of the American tradition. The concept of Cultural Revolution "affords the intellectual means, the conceptual framework, the theoretical link that ties together all the disparate, conflicting and contending trends within the Negro movement as a whole in order to transform the movement from a mere rebellion into a revolutionary movement that can "shape actions to ideas, to fit the world into a theoretic frame" (112). Hence, "Cultural Revolution means an ideological and organizational approach to American social change by revolutionizing the administration, the organization, the functioning, and the social purpose of the entire American apparatus of cultural communication and placing it under public ownership" (112).

According to Cruse, African Americans must assume this initiative both because they are "the only ethnic group in America who has the need, the motivation and the historical prerogative to demand such changes," and "because racial equality cannot be achieved unless the Negro rebellion adopts revolutionary tactics which can enforce structural changes in the administration of certain sections of the national economy" (112). This would challenge American free enterprise at its weakest point. And, because the race question is a cultural question, "the concept of Cultural Revolution becomes an intellectual means of introducing a new set of ideas into American social theory" (113). African American culture is the basis of what is unique in American culture; it is the basis of all "popular culture" in America. For white America to acknowledge this would demand that African Americans "be culturally glorified and elevated socially, economically and politically" (116).

Consequently, for Cruse, a cultural program must address both the aesthetics and the economics of cultural production in America. This is the meaning and purpose of Cultural Revolution, and "without such a revolution the Negro movement has no point of departure from which to compel the necessary social impact to effect structural changes within the American social system" (117).

How might this Cultural Revolution come about? Cruse seems to offer little insight on this point. Other than to assert that African American intellectuals would have a special role to play in this Cultural Revolution, Cruse is silent on the organizational aspects of the Cultural Revolution. As pointed out by sociologist Thomas L. Blair (1977),

> [t]here is little evidence to support Cruse's assertion that the cultural sector is the weakest area of American capitalism. And how is his proposal for a cultural media revolution to come about? All that emerges is a plan for the democratization of relations between competing ethnic groups and for increased access by blacks to the mass media. What Cruse seems to be after is the creation of a new elite corps of black middle-class cultural administrators who would be more sensitive and responsible to their communities than has been the case up to now. Insofar as the system remains the same and blacks are last in line for media rewards (and Cruse gives no indication how the system and its allocation of rewards might be changed by black media men and women), then the black cultural revolution amounts to nothing more than token integration at best. And at worst it would increase widespread fears that the Establishment would use black media personnel to absorb black protest and disseminate a distorted set of images and values (145).

100

Thus, on closer examination, Cruse's Cultural Revolution turns out to be not so revolutionary after all. In fact, Cruse's proposal is nothing more than cultural nationalism.

But these ideas, tactics, and proposals have proven severely limited in the sense that they are not fundamentally revolutionary and in the sense that they fail to address the psychological component of the African American experience. Because the African American is in a unique situation, the next step is revolutionary social action. But such action must conceive a new revolutionary theory that goes beyond the models of anti-colonialism, liberalism, socialism, communism, and all past social revolutions in method, subject, meaning, intent, targets, and objects. This is because African Americans are in the most developed capitalist nation in the world, and therefore there are no historical guides or experiences within the Western tradition. Consequently, African Americans must create a new revolutionary synthesis. However, the new revolutionary theory must contain all the elements of political class struggle in terms of meaning, purpose, and method. These elements require class-consciousness, organization for conflict, control of the political system, and disposition of the existing government. Additionally, the new revolutionary theory must overcome the obstacles that currently prohibit African Americans from forming a political class.

Therefore, the new revolutionary theory must be therapeutic in the sense that it functions as a healer discovering the meanings of symptoms--symptoms both psychological and social--and bringing about modifications in social behavior by providing a model social group. The revolutionary theory is, as political scientist James Glass (1974) understood, political philosophy to be, a therapy. Glass equates the revolutionary theory to the shaman who uses his incantations as a curative for public ailments. The revolutionary theory, like the shaman, attempts to transform consciousness by introducing a vision of regeneration. According to Glass, "The philosophical incantation, as psychological cure, possesses a meaning which transcends formal classifications, whether 'descriptive' or normative; it enters into consciousness, ideally as a transformer of meaning, as a perceptual magic that banishes the historical causes of suffering and founds an entirely novel gestalt" (193). This is also analogous to psychiatrist David Cooper's (1970) understanding of revolution in an advanced, industrial society. For Cooper, the revolutionary act must recondition the person, allowing him to transcend "the major bits of his micro- and macro-social conditioning in the direction of the spontaneous self-assertion of full personal autonomy, which in itself is a decisive act of counter violence against the system" (62). Hence, according to Cooper, revolution must help people "to realize how the power of the ruling elite and its bureaucracy is nothing, nothing but their refused and externalized power. Then it is a matter of recuperation of that power, and the recuperative strategy is quite simple: act against the "rules" and the act itself converts the illusory power in them into real power in us" (78).

Thus, the task of the new revolutionary theory is a communal one.

Its regenerative vision is introduced into the consciousness of the audience, the African American community, in therapeutic fashion; it addresses the unconscious dimension that is responsible for the individual's suffering, a necessary component to any therapy. The therapeutic objective is to restore the wounded psyche by altering those traits associated with a depraved society; it must sever the self from its alienated existence and restore ego consciousness. It is only through this contrast that the "new" human being and human community emerge.

As a therapeutic measure, the new revolutionary theory must discover the meaning of symptoms and connect them to their cause. As presented in an earlier chapter of this discussion, most explanations of race relations have focused on symptomatic elements as if they were causes. However, it has been argued that social status is the principle cause that determines race relations. Social status creates a frame of reference, a mental construction responsible for the organization, arrangement, or adjustment of ideas and beliefs. Social status is a point of reference from which other ideas and beliefs are interpreted or assigned meaning. It assists us in explaining things to ourselves, in understanding, in guiding the focus of attention, and in determining what we will (or will not) notice. Psychologist Daniel Goleman (1985) refers to this way of thinking as a "schema" that acts like "a censor when it suppresses available information on the ground that it is not just irrelevant, but forbidden" (106). Consequently, the schema, like a screening device, divides, sifts, selects, diverts, and conceals information from our attention and therefore keeps it out of consciousness. The result is repetition.

Therefore, social status as a frame of reference or schema directs not just what we think about others but also what we think about ourselves. This is what sociologist Charles Cooley (1960) calls the "looking-glass self." According to Cooley, we are largely a reflection of the opinions and estimates that we believe others hold of us. Thus, we are what we think of ourselves; what others think of us; and we are a collective view, a collective self, and a social product. As such, we are susceptible to social control that establishes conformity by using the status designation as the frame or schema to condition our reactions and behaviors.

Hence, race relations are social constructions, schemas, or frames, from which we think about the other, interpret the other, and assign meaning to the other. It is also a schema from which we think about ourselves, interpret ourselves, and assign meaning to ourselves. Race relations are predicated on the shared schema or frame of a collective self. And therefore, status based on race carries social meaning, and its meaning establishes the context of social interaction. As a result, the social meaning of racial status scripts behaviors and actions. Thus, the social context of race relations defines for each actor his social role.

Accordingly, the social role determines, in part, what and how one exists in actuality. The social role, as part of a schema or frame, establishes whether one will be the subject or object of experience, that is, whether one will have the freedom of self-determination or the un-freedom of being other-determined. Therefore, the lowly status of African Americans makes of them objects of experience, and their attempts at self-determination are constantly negated and thwarted. Social reality, as produced by human actions, turns back on humans and conditions them. Thus, the roles of subject and object are reproduced and reinforced.

Given this understanding, we may discover the meaning of the many symptoms associated with lowly status and racial oppression. As demonstrated throughout this discussion, the lowly status ascribed African Americans as a consequence of slavery has engendered a process of social adversity, social crisis, and social demoralization. Each phase of this process produced behaviors that were symptomatic of the original position ascribed African Americans. In other words, the symptoms of lowly status and racial oppression are consequences of the schema or frame of racial status, and African Americans exist and do as the schema or frame of racial status allows them to be and do. Because the schema or frame is unconscious, it resists revision, perpetuates repetitive patterns of behaviors, and results in bizarre perceptions and actions.

Such schemas or frames can only be overcome by insight or awareness, and this is the task of a therapeutic revolutionary theory. It must do schema or frame repair; it must confront information that has been resisted. The therapeutic revolutionary theory must perform what Brazilian educator Paulo Freire (1968) describes as "critical intervention," in which the "oppressed must confront reality critically, simultaneously objectifying and acting upon that reality" (37). It must unveil the world of oppression and deal with the problem of the oppressed consciousness, taking account of the behavior of the oppressed and their view of the world. Thus, critical intervention leads to critical consciousness, which grasps true causality and submits it to analysis. Here begins the discovery that the oppressed are hosts of the oppressor; the oppressor is objectified and discovered outside of themselves. This is the awakening of consciousness, and here begins the journey toward liberation.

Therefore, it is the responsibility of the African American intelligentsia to perform the therapeutic intervention necessary for the development of African American class-consciousness. Like the priests and medicine men from the West African traditions, the African American intelligentsia must "assume the task of interpreting the universe and codifying and rationalizing cultural values." It must also treat the illnesses and ailments through cures and advice that fend off the evil spirits of lowly status, social adversity, social crisis, and social demoralization and restore equanimity to African American life (Banks 1996, 3-4). Like the conjurer during plantation slavery, the African American intelligentsia must "function as the healer of the sick, the interpreter of the unknown, the comforter of the sorrowing, the supernatural avenger of wrong and the one who . . . [expresses] the longing, disappointment and resentment of a stolen and oppressed people" (Blassingame 1972, 33).

The conflicts between intellectualism and activism cannot be allowed to stand in the way of African American intellectuals' responsibility to the African American masses. Past tensions concerning scholarly ideals and partisan activism have no practical significance within the contemporary social environment. Both activists and intellectuals have distinct roles to play within the African American social experience. The two together constitute praxis, that is, reflection and action, and when either is deprived of its constitutive function, both suffer. As pointed out by Brazilian educator Paulo Freire (1970), "When a word is deprived of its dimension of action, reflection automatically suffers as well; and the word is changed into idle chatter, into verbalism, into an alienated and alienating 'blah'" (75-76). And when "action is emphasized exclusively, to the detriment of reflection, the word is converted into activism. The latter--action for action's sake--negates true praxis . . ." (76). Therefore, intellectuals and activists are necessary to the formation of praxis, since, as Freire points out, "a revolution is achieved with neither verbalism nor activism, but rather with praxis, that is, with reflection and action directed at the structures to be transformed" (120). Hence, the revolution needs thinkers and doers.

Furthermore, questions and conflicts over the diversity of individual reactions and responses to the racial situation among African American intellectuals must be recognized for what they are: a fundamental dimension of oppressive action or, more specifically, divide and rule. African American responses to the racial situation have never been uniform. During slavery, the only consensus was that slavery had to be abolished. However, the method for accomplishing this goal was debated; some argued for violence against slaveholders, others argued for governmental action, and some argued for separation. So among the "small group of educated blacks, none was reluctant to attack the ideas (and often the motives) of those who held different views about the most effective means of achieving and exercising liberty and freedom" (Banks 1996, 227).

After Emancipation and through the first half of the twentieth century, African American intellectuals clashed over the most effective approach to remedying racial discrimination. Leaders such as Booker T. Washington, W. E. B. DuBois, and Marcus Garvey offered different agendas to the African American community. During the Harlem Renaissance, creative artists and "scholars argued about goals, tactics, and values. Overall, the specter of a hostile white establishment tended to forge a confederacy of black opinion about racial issues" (Banks 1996, 228). During the civil rights era, few, if any, African American intellectuals "disputed the fundamental goals of nondiscrimination and greater opportunities for blacks, but differences about emphases and tactics quickly surfaced" (Banks 1996, 228).

However, the post-civil rights period has witnessed no single issue to mobilize the African American intellectual community. According to William M. Banks, professor of African American studies,

Because liberals had been their strongest allies in the battle against discrimination, most black thinkers remained loyal to the liberal sector of the political spectrum, despite their frustration with the timidity and unreliability of the liberal camp. But several thoughtful and combative blacks rejected liberal ideology and championed social and economic conservatism as the best hope for black freedom, justice, and equality in the post-civil rights period (228).

Thus, the discussion of racial inequality has shifted from a group-centered focus to an emphasis on individual behavior. Consequently, as pointed out by Banks (1996), "a growing number of black intellectuals resist the idea that race is a defining element in their social and psychological world . . . they feel that they, individually, are less affected by racial boundaries, that race does not weigh as heavily on their experience as it may have on that of their predecessors" (237).

Instead, for many African American intellectuals the focus is on individual responsibility for overcoming disadvantaged backgrounds and social barriers, of which they are stellar examples. High unemployment, low educational achievement, high rates of out-of-wedlock births, and rising crime rates are attributable to the culture of the African American poor rather than to discrimination and economic injustice.

But on closer examination, the discussion among African American intellectuals is the classic case of divide and rule. Supporters of the status quo, in order to maintain their own hegemony, create, deepen, exploit, and sustain rifts among African Americans. In general, the contemporary status quo view of issues and tensions associated with race focus on African American attitudes and conduct that need to change. The waning of overt racial discrimination suggests that whatever difficulties African Americans face is a consequence of their own attitudes and behavior, a failure on their behalf to adapt to the demands of this nation. Special assistance or preferential treatment simply corrupts the character of African Americans. In support of this thesis, conservative African American intellectuals--Thomas Sowell, Shelby Steele, Glenn Loury, Stanley Crouch, and Stephen Carter among others--are cited by the mainstream as proof that African Americans have played the victim role too long and must take responsibility for themselves rather than blaming society. The assumption is that each individual must save himself. But individuals cannot save themselves. Salvation in the racial context can only be achieved with others.

Thus, by focalizing racial issues, that is, isolating racial problems from their totality, this faction has increased alienation among African Americans and distorted their perception of reality, ultimately making it much easier for their numbers to be divided. Racial problems are not individual problems but parts of a totality, which include many different areas and regions across the nation. Isolating racial problems as individual problems separate from the problem of racial oppression weakens African

American resistance and unification. It diverts attention from the real problem by focusing on its symptoms. This focalized view of racial problems opens the door to manipulation, and manipulation becomes another instrument by which dominant elites maintain the status quo. Because African Americans lack class-consciousness and are therefore divided, the deceits and false promises of manipulation find fertile ground. This manipulation successfully blocks the emergence of class-consciousness by anesthetizing African Americans, keeping them from thinking, and distracting them from the true cause of their problem. It splinters African Americans into groups of individuals who only seek benefits for themselves, hence aiding in the strategy of division. Therefore, preventing unification of African Americans serves the interests of the dominant elite; their power requires that African Americans be divided.

So, the African American intelligentsia of scholars and creative artists must unveil the world of racial oppression; they must initiate the unveiling on behalf of African Americans. They must de-mythicize and de-ideologize racial oppression so that African Americans may come to know the why and how of their racial oppression. It is the task of the African American intelligentsia to expose the oppressor housed within African Americans, because as long as the oppressor housed in African Americans is stronger than they are, their fear of freedom will lead them to denounce revolutionary action. The unity of African Americans involves solidarity regardless of social status, and this unity requires class-consciousness; however, becoming conscious of being an oppressed individual must precede class-consciousness.

The African American consciousness is a consciousness of oppression. Born into slavery and nurtured on lowly status, this oppressed consciousness compels every expression in the lives of African Americans. It is the manifestation of what they think and believe; it colors what they are to themselves and what they are to others. In an absurd, twisted logic, the African American experience and condition are the social creation of a distorted, white, American oppressor consciousness that has been incorporated and appendaged to the oppressed, African-American consciousness. In this situation, African Americans are double victims of white American oppression: (1) They are what white Americans believe about them, and (2) they believe what white Americans believe about them. In this way, African Americans are victims both of an oppressive social reality and of their own beliefs. Hence, African Americans mistakenly seek the cause of their lowly status and racial oppression in the symptoms, such as cultural deficiencies, racial bias, and structural disadvantages and obstacles. In their confusion, they think power into these effects. They war against their own reflection, the veils that condition their being. They are burdened by their own minds. Subconsciously, they give power to these outer conditions and effects, and in doing so are robbed by their own false beliefs. Diverted by the blind spots created by the racial schema, African Americans cannot recognize that only by transforming his consciousness can a person transform his world.

So, the status ascribed to African Americans is set down on a wrong that has produced immense revolutionary possibilities. As a consequence first of being possessed as a thing and then of being subjected to a fraud and crime enforced by the political apparatus, African Americans have been persistently denied fulfillment and atonement. Subsequently, African Americans have been at the forefront for social change in America. The next phase of the struggle must be revolutionary in nature with a therapeutic component. The responsibility for this falls to the African American intelligentsia, who must perform the therapeutic intervention necessary for the development of political class-consciousness and political class struggle.

Here, in capsule form, is the basis for a new revolutionary theory with a therapeutic function. It contains the seeds for discovering the meaning of both psychological and social symptoms; it addresses that subconscious dimension responsible for suffering. Only with these factors can consciousness be transformed, public aliments cured, the wounded psyche restored, and a vision of regeneration presented. Only then can political class-consciousness and political class struggle become a possibility capable of transforming that potent rebelliousness of African Americans into social revolution.

Conclusion

In this rather short study, I have explored the significance of social status as the primary variable for understanding American race relation. I have demonstrated that lowly status, when supported by racial antipathy, leads to an array of spiraling social problems. Supported by historical evidence that is tied to psychological and sociological concepts, the study presents a different, though not novel, perspective from which to evaluate American race relations.

American race relations are closely tied up with social status. Race relations are therefore status relations and reflect the economic and social forces that are responsible for their development. What appears as distorted, pathological behaviors and thoughts among African Americans is actually due to the fact that African Americans are marginalized within American society and generally suppressed by racial discrimination at the bottom of the social status gradient.

As a result, African Americans are predisposed to specific psychosocial impediments. First, they are subjected to severe social adversities within the American social, economic, and political systems. The position of African Americans in American life has made it difficult and laborious for African Americans to overcome the many disadvantages and barriers to social, economic, and political advancement. Second, prolonged social adversity has made African Americans highly susceptible to feelings of social crisis. Mentally debilitated by their predicament, African Americans are overwhelmed by emotion and stress, which severely retard their social functioning. Finally, with shattered morale and shaken confidence, the African American is socially demoralized and given over to random, inconsistent, irrelevant, and irresponsible behavior.

But the situation of American race relations raises serious questions about the grandiose assertions of American democracy, equality, liberty, and opportunity. The situation of American race relations makes these proclamations a lie. American political democracy is a sham when viewed through the lens of race relations; equality is a joke when evaluated under the historical evidence. Liberty is bogus when scrutinized through the African American experience, and opportunity is a delusion when professed under conditions of racial prejudice, discrimination, and oppression. The meaning of American nationhood is called into question by the situation of race relations.

Because race relations are status relations, it is a difficult and complicated problem of power. Social power organizes society, and the dynamics of societal organization are determined and controlled by the dominant political class, which holds the power to create, sustain, or prevent social change. The exercise of power reflects the economic, political, and social interests of the dominant political class. Therefore, a counter-class, the antithesis of the dominant political class, is necessarily the only vehicle by which right can be restored.

But this can only be accomplished by awakening class-consciousness among African Americans. And to do this requires a revolutionary theory that functions as a therapy in addition to being a method of political class struggle. Class-consciousness will not arise through some metaphysical intervention or through some natural, spontaneous historical evolution. The development of class-consciousness requires an intervention by that segment of the African American intelligentsia that is objectively situated outside, or at least on the fringe, of the social restraints induced by social crisis and social demoralization and who comprehend the socio-political situation in its totality devoid of particular, individual, short term, and short-sighted interests.

Appendix

Table1. Poverty Rate by Age and Race: 2001

	Total	Under 18	65 and over
Total	11.7	16.3	10.1
Black	22.7	30.2	21.9
White	7.8	9.5	8.1

Source: U.S. Census Bureau, Annual Demographic Supplement to the March 2002 Current Population Survey.

Table 2. Family Income by Family Type and Race of Householder: 2001

	Less than $25,000	$25,000- $34,999	$35,000- $49,000	$50,000- $74,000	$75,000 and over
Married Couple					
Black	18.8	11.6	17.1	25.5	26.9
White	11.8	9.6	15.0	23.5	40.1
Female					
Black	58.1	15.7	12.6	9.0	4.7
White	41.1	17.2	17.6	13.5	10.5
Male					
Black	37.6	18.9	17.9	14.6	10.9
White	24.5	16.8	20.1	19.5	19.1

Source: U.S. Census Bureau, Annual Demographic Supplement to the March 2002 Current Population Survey.

Table 3. Educational Attainment by Sex and Race: 2002

	High School Graduate	Some College Associate degree	Bachelor's degree
Male			
Black	34.8	27.3	16.4
White	31.5	25.2	31.7
Female			
Black	33.3	28.2	17.5
White	34.3	27.3	27.3

Source: U.S. Census Bureau, Annual Demographic Supplement to the March 2002 Current Population Survey.

Table 4. Earnings of Workers 18 Years Old and Over, by Educational Attainment, Race, and Sex: 2001

Race/Sex	Earnings Mean	Not a H.S. Graduate	High School	Some College/Assoc.Degree	Bachelor's Degree	Advanced Degree
Whites	$38,844	$19,120	$27,000	$31,482	$51,631	$74,398
Males	$45,071	$22,006	$33,545	$38,501	$65,046	$92,304
Females	$27,240	$14,197	$20,866	$24,387	$36,698	$51,499
Blacks	$27,031	$17,248	$21,743	$26,907	$40,165	$55,771
Males	$30,502	$18,543	$25,037	$31,084	$46,511	$67,007
Females	$24,036	$15,912	$18,683	$23,511	$35,448	$48,080

Source: U.S. Census Bureau, Current Population Survey.

References

Abramson, Paul R. 1983. Political Attitudes in America: Formation and Change. San Francisco: W. H. Freeman and Company.

Alexander, Peter. 1987. Racism Resistance and Revolution. London: Bookmarks.

Allen, Robert. 1969. Black Awakening in Capitalist America. Garden City, NY: Doubleday.

------. 1974. Reluctant Reformers: Racism and Social Reform Movements in the United States. Washington, DC: Howard University Press.

Anderson, Elijah. 1999. Code of the Street: Decency, Violence, and the Moral Life of the InnerCity. New York: W. W. Norton.

Auletta, Kenneth. 1982. The Underclass. New York: Random House.

Banefield, Edward. 1970. The Unheavenly City. Boston: Little Brown.

Banks, William M. 1996. Black Intellectuals: Race and Responsibility in American Life. NewYork: W. W. Norton.

Baran, Paul A. and Paul M. Sweezy. 1966. Monopoly Capital. New York: Monthly ReviewPress.

Barrera, Mario. 1979. Race and Class in the Southwest: A Theory of Racial Inequality. NotreDame, IN: University of Notre Dame Press.

Bell, Derrick. 1992. Faces at the Bottom of the Well: The Permanence of Racism. New York:Basic Books.

Bellah, Robert N., et al. 1985. Habits of the Heart: Individualism and Commitment in American Life. New York: Harper and Row.

Berry, Mary Frances and John W. Blassingame. (1982). Long

References

Memory: The Black Experiencein America. New York: Oxford University Press.

------. (1992). "Blacks and the Politics of Redemption." In A Turbulent Voyage. Ed. Floyd W. Hayes, III, 597-634. San Diego, CA: Collegiate Press.

Billingsley, Andrew. 1992. Climbing Jacob's Ladder: The Enduring Legacy of African American Families. New York: Touchstone.

Blair, Thomas L. 1977. Retreat to the Ghetto: The End of a Dream? New York: Hill and Wang.

Blassingame, John W. 1972. The Slave Community: Plantation Life in the Antebellum South. New York: Oxford University Press.

Blauner, Robert. 1972. Racial Oppression in America. New York: Harper and Row.

Bloom, Jack M. 1987. Class, Race, and the Civil Rights Movement. Bloomington, IN: Indiana University Press.

Bogardus, Emory S. 1960. The Development of Social Thought. 4th ed. New York: DavidMcKay Company.

Camus, Albert. 1956. The Rebel: An Essay on Man in Revolt. New York: Vintage Books.

Carmichael, Stokely, and Charles Hamilton. 1967. Black Power. New York: Random House.

Clark, Dovie K. 1942. "Peter Humpheries Clark." Negro History Bulletin 6: 176-77.

Clark, Kenneth B. 1965. Dark Ghetto. New York: Harper and Row.

------. 1974. Pathos of Power. New York: Harper Torchbooks.

Cone, James H. [1970] 1990. A Black Theology of Liberation. New York: Orbis Books.

Cooper, David. 1970. The Death of the Family. New York: Vintage Books.

Cox, Oliver C. [1948] 1970. Caste, Class, and Race: A Study in Social Dynamics. New York: Modern Reader.

------. 1987. "Significance of Rural Culture for Race Relations." In Race, Class, and the World System: The Sociology of Oliver C. Cox, eds. Herbert M. Hunter and Sameer Y. Abraham. New York: Monthly Review Press.

Cruse, Harold. 1967. The Crisis of the Negro Intellectual. New York: William Morrow.

------. 1968. Rebellion or Revolution. New York: William Morrow.

------. 1987. Plural but Equal: A Critical Study of Blacks and Minorities in America's Plural Society. New York: William Morrow.

Davis, Allison, Burleigh Gardner, and Mary Gardner. 1941. Deep South. Chicago: University of Chicago Press.

Degler, Carl N. 1970. Out of Our Past: The Forces that Shaped Modern America. Rev. ed. New York: Harper Colophon.

DeLue, Steven M. 1997. Political Thinking, Political Theory, and Civil Society. Boston: Allyn and Bacon.

Dixon, Samuel L. 1979. Working with People in Crisis: Theory and

REFERENCES

Practice. St. Louis: C. V. Mosby.

Dollard, John. 1957. Caste and Class in a Southern Town. 3rd ed. Garden City, NY: Doubleday.

Domhoff, G. William. 1978. The Powers that Be: Process of Ruling Class Domination in America. New York: Vintage Books.

Draper, Theodore. 1960. American Communism and Soviet Russia: The Formative Period. New York: Viking Press.

D'Souza, Dinesh. 1995. The End of Racism: Principles for a Multicultural Society. New York: The Free Press.

Dubin, S. C. 1987. "Symbolic Slavery: Black Representations in Popular Culture." Social Problems 34(2): 122-40.

Dye, Thomas R. and Harmon Zeigler. 2000. The Irony of Democracy: An Uncommon Introduction to American Politics. New York: Harcourt Brace.

Easton, Hosea. 1969. "A Treatise on the Intellectual Character and Civil and Political Condition of the Colored People of the United States; and the Prejudice Exercised Toward Them." In Negro Protest Pamphlets, ed. Dorothy Porter. New York: Arno Press.

Edelman, Murray. 1971. Politics as Symbolic Action. Chicago: Markham Publishing.

Ellison, Ralph. [1947] 1972. Invisible Man. New York: Vintage Books.

Equiano, Olaudah. 1972. "The Interesting Narrative of the Life of Olaudah Equiano, or Gustavus Vassa, the African." In Black Writers of America: A Comprehensive Anthology, eds. Richard Barksdale and Keneth Kinnamon. New York: The Macmillan Company.

Fanon, Frantz. 1968. The Wretched of the Earth. Trans. Constance Farrington. New York: Grove Press.

Feagin, Joe C. 1991. "The Continuing Significance of Race: Antiblack Discrimination in Public Places." American Sociological Review 56: 101-116.

Fehrenbacher, Don E. 1978. The Dred Scott Case: Its Significance in American Law and Politics. New York: Oxford University Press.

Fields, Barbara J. 1982. "Ideology and Race in American History." In Region, Race, and Reconstruction, eds. J. M. Kousser and J. M. McPherson. New York: Oxford University Press.

Foner, Philip S. 1974. Organized Labor and the Black Worker 1619-1973. New York: Praeger.

------. 1977. American Socialism and Black Americans: From the Age of Jackson to World War II. Westport, CT: Greenwood Press.

Franklin, John Hope, and Alfred A. Moss. 1994. From Slavery to Freedom: A History of African Americans. 7th ed. New York: McGraw-Hill.

Frazier, E. Franklin. 1962. Black Bourgeoisie: The Rise of a New Middle Class in the United States. New York: Collier Books.

------. **1964.** The Negro Church in America. New York: Schocer.

Fredrickson, George M. 1995. Black Liberation: A Comparative

References

History of Black Ideologies in the United States and South Africa. New York: Oxford University Press.

------. 2002. Racism: A Short History. Princeton, NJ: Princeton University Press.

Freire, Paulo. 1970. Pedagogy of the Oppressed. Trans. Myra Bergman Ramos. New York: Seabury Press.

------. **1973.** Education for Critical Consciousness. New York: Continuum.

Gelpi, Donald L, ed. 1989. Beyond Individualism. Notre Dame, IN: University of Notre Dame Press.

Genovese, Eugene D. 1969. The World the Slaveholders Made: Two Essays in Interpretation. New York: Pantheon Books.

Glass, James M. 1974. "The Philosopher and the Shaman: The Political Vision as Incantation." Political Theory 2: 193

Goffman, Erving. 1963. Stigma: Notes on the Management of Spoiled Identity. Englewood Cliffs, NJ: Prentice-Hall.

Goleman, Daniel. 1985. Vital Lies; Simple Truths: The Psychology of Self-Deception. New York: Simon and Schuster.

Gordon, R. A. 1987. "SES Versus IQ in the Race-IQ Delinquency Model." International Journal of Sociology and Social Policy 7: 30-96.

Grier, William H., and Price M. Cobbs. 1968. Black Rage. New York: Bantam.

Grigsby, Daryl R. 1987. For the People: Black Socialist in the United States, Africa, and theCaribbean. San Diego: Asante Publications.

Gross, Bertram. 1980. Friendly Fascism: The New Face of Power in America. Boston: South End Press.

Hacker, Andrew. 1992. Two Nations: Black and White, Separate, Hostile, Unequal. New York: Charles Scribner's Sons.

Hamilton, Alexander, James Madison, and John Jay. 1961. The Federalist Papers. New York: Mentor.

Hernstein, Richard J., and Charles A. Murray. 1994. The Bell Curve: Intelligence and Class Structure in American Life. New York: The Free Press.

------. 1971. "IQ." The Atlantic Monthly, September.

Higginbotham, A. Leon. 1978. In the Matter of Color: Race and the American Legal Process: The Colonial Period. New York: Oxford University Press.

Hill, Herbert. 1985. Black Labor and the American Legal System. Madison, WI: University of Wisconsin Press.

Huckfeldt, Robert, and Carol W. Kohfeld. 1989. Race and the Decline of Class in AmericanPolitics. Urbana, IL: University of Illinois Press.

Human Rights Watch. 2000. "United States: Punishment and Prejudice: Racial Disparaties inThe War on Drugs." 12(2): May. http://www.hrw.org/reports/2000/usa/

------. 2002. Human Rights Watch Report 2002: United States. http:

118

References

//www.hrw.org/wr2k2/us

Jensen, Arthur. 1969. "How Much Can We Boost IQ and Scholastic Achievement?" Harvard Educational Review 39: 1-123.

------. 1973. Educability and Group Differences. New York: Harper and Row.

Joint Center for Political and Economic Studies. 1999. "Living Arrangements of Children." July. http://www.jointcenter.org/database/factsht/livarg.htm

------. 1999. "Trends in Poverty. September. http://jointcenter.org/database/factsht/trendnpov.htm

Kamenka, Eugene, ed. 1982. Community as a Social Ideal. London: Eduard Arnold.

Kardiner, Abram, and Lionel Ovesey. 1951. The Mark of Oppression: Explorations in the Personality of the American Negro. Cleveland: Meridian.

Kessler, Sidney H. 1952. "The Negro in the Knights of Labor." Journal of Negro History 37: 250-82.

Knox, T. M., trans. [1952] 1981. Hegel's Philosophy of Right. New York: Oxford University Press.

Kuykendall, Ronald A. 2002. "African Blood Brotherhood, Independent Marxist During the Harlem Renaissance." The Western Journal of Black Studies 26(1): 16-21.

Laing, R. D. 1969. Self and Others. New York: Pantheon Books.

------. **1967.** The Politics of Experience. New York: Ballentine Books.

LaPiere, Richard T. 1954. A Theory of Social Control. New York: McGraw-Hill.

Lewis Mumford Center. 2002. "Choosing Segregation: Racial Imbalance in American Public Schools, 1999-2000." March. http://mumford1.dyndns.org/cen2000/SchoolsPop/SPReport/page1.html

------. 2001. "Ethnic Diversity Grows, Neighborhood Integration Lags Behind." December. http://mumford1.dyndns.org/cen2000/WholePop/Wpreport/page1.html

Logan, Rayford W. [1954] 1965. The Betrayal of the Negro: From Rutherford B. Hayes toWoodrow Wilson. New York: Collier-Macmillan.

Lukacs, Georg. 1971. History and Class Consciousness: Studies in Marxist Dialectics. Trans. Rodney Livingstone. Cambridge, MA: The MIT Press.

MacIntyre, Alasdair. 1984. After Virtue: A Study in Moral Theory. 2nd ed. Notre Dame, IN: University of Notre Dame Press.

Macquarrie, John. 1968. Martin Heidegger. Richmond, VA: John Knox Press.

McClendon, W. H. 1983. "The Foundation of Black Culture." Black Scholar 14: 18-20.

McConahay, J. B., and J. C. Hough. 1976. "Symbolic Racism." Journal of Social Issues 32(2): 23-45

McIntosh, Peggy. 1988. White Privilege and Male Privilege: A

References

Personal Account of Coming To See Correspondences through Work in Women's Studies. Wellesley, MA: Wellesley College Center for Research on Women.

Marable, Manning. 1985. Black American Politics: From the Washington Marches to Jesse Jackson. London: Verso.

Martin, Tony. 1976. Race First: The Ideological and Organizational Struggles of Marcus Garvey and the Universal Negro Improvement Association. Westport, CT: Greenwood Press.

Massey, Douglass S. and Nancy A. Denton. 1987. "Trends in Residential Segregation of Blacks, Hispanics, and Asians: 1970-1980." Sociological Review 52: 179

-------. 1988. "Suburbanization and Segregation in U.S. Metropolitan Areas." American Journal of Sociology 94: 529

Mason, Philip. 1970. Patterns of Domination. London: Oxford University Press.

Meier, August, and Elliot Rudwick. 1970. From Plantation to Ghetto. Rev.ed. New York: Hill and Wang.

------. 1969. "Black Violence in the 20th Century: A Study in Rhetoric and Retaliation." In Violence in America: Historical and Comparative Perspectives. Eds. Hugh Davis Graham and Ted Robert Gurr. New York: Bantam.

Miami Theory Collective. 1991. Community at Loose Ends. Minneapolis: University of Minnesota Press.

Miller, Sally M. 1971. "The Socialist Party and the Negro, 1901-1921." Journal of NegroHistory 56: 220-239.

Morris, Milton D. 1992. "Democratic Politics and Black Subordination." In A Turbulent Voyage. Ed. Floyd W. Hayes, III, 582-596. San Diego, CA: Collegiate Press.

Mosca, Gaetano. 1939. The Ruling Class. Ed. Arthur Livingston. Trans. Hannah D. Kahn.New York: McGraw-Hill.

Moynihan, Daniel P. 1965. The Negro Family: The Case for National Action. Washington, DC: U. S. Department of Labor.

Murray, Charles. 1984. Losing Ground: American Social Policy 1950-1980. New York: Basic.

Myrdal, Gunnar. 1944. An American Dilemma. New York: Pantheon.

Naison, Mark. 1983. Communists in Harlem During the Depression. New York: Grove Press.

Parenti, Michael. 1995. Democracy for the Few. 6th ed. New York: St. Martin's Press.

Patterson, Orlando. 1982. Slavery and Social Death: A Comparative Study. Cambridge, MA: Harvard University Press.

Pease, William H. and Jane Pease. 1963. Black Utopia: Negro Communal Experiments in America. Madison, WI: The State Historical Society of Wisconsin.

Piven, Frances Fox, and Richard A. Cloward. 1977. Poor People's Movements: Why They Succeed, How They Fail. New York: Vintage.

Poussaint, Alvin F. and Amy Alexander. (2000). Lay My Burden

References

Down: Unraveling Suicide and the Mental Health Crisis among African Americans. Boston: Beacon Press.

Prager, Jeffrey. 1987. "American Political Culture and the Shifting Meaning of Race. Ethnic and Racial Studies 10: 62-81.

Robinson, Cedric J. 1983. Black Marxism: The Making of the Black Radical Tradition. London: Zed Press.

Robinson, Donald L. 1971. Slavery in the Structure of American Politics 1765-1820. New York: Harcourt, Brace, Jovanovich.

Robinson, Randall. 2000. The Debt: What America Owes to Blacks. New York: Dutton.

Rogers, Harrell R., and Charles R. Bullock. 1972. Law and Social Change: Civil Rights Laws and Their Consequences. New York: McGraw-Hill.

Roper, Moses. 1972. "A Narrative of the Adventures and Escape of Moses Roper, from American Slavery." In Black Writers of America: A Comprehensive Anthology, eds. Richard Barksdale and Keneth Kinnamon. New York: The Macmillan Company.

Rowen, Carl. 1996. The Coming Race War in America: A Wake-up Call. Boston: Little, Brown and Company

Rueter, Theodore. 1995. "The New Black Conservatives." In The Politics of Race: African Americans and the Political System, ed. Theodore Rueter. Armonk, NY: M. E. Sharpe.

Ryan, William. 1971. Blaming the Victim. New York: Vintage Books.

Southern Poverty Law Center. 2002. Intelligence Project. http://www.tolerance.org.

Schmitt, Richard. 1988. "A New Hypothesis about the Relations of Class, Race, and Gender: Capitalism as a Dependent System." Social Theory and Practice 14(3): 345-65.

Schopenhauer, Arthur. 1962. The Will to Live: Selected Writings of Arthur Schopenhauer. Ed. Richard Taylor. New York: Anchor Books.

Starkloff, Carl F. 1989. "Beyond the Melting Pot: An Essay in Cultural Transcendence." In Beyond Individualism, ed. D. L. Gelpi. Notre Dame, IN: University of Notre Dame Press.

Stuckey, Sterling. 1987. Slave Culture: Nationalist Theory and the Foundations of BlackAmerica. New York: Oxford University Press.

Taylor, Charles. 1984. "Hegel: History and Politics." In Liberalism and Its Critics, ed. M. J. Sandel. New York: New York University Press.

de Tocqueville, Alexis. 1969. Democracy in America. New York: Doubleday.

Thomas, Richard W. 1991. "The Historical Roots of Contemporary Urban Black Self-Help in the United States. In Contemporary Urban America: Problems, Issues, and Alternatives ed. Marvel Lang. Lanham, MD: University Press of America.

Thompson, John B. 1990. Ideology and Modern Culture. Stanford, CA: Stanford University Press.

Turner, Margery, Michael Fix, and Raymond J. Struyk. 1991.

"Opportunities Denied, Opportunites Diminished: Discrimination in Hiring." Washington, DC: The Urban Institute.

U.S. Census Bureau. 2003. "The Black Population in the United States: March 2002." www.census.gov/prod/2003pubs/p20-541

Vincent, Theodore G. 1971. Black Power and the Garvey Movement. San Francisco: Ramparts Press.

Wallerstein, Immanuel. 1974. The Modern World-System: Capitalist Agriculture and the Origins of the European World-Economy. New York: Academic Press.

Walters, Ronald W. 1977. "Marxism-Leninism and the Black Revolution: A Critical Essay." In Black Separatism and Social Reality: Rhetoric and Reason. Ed. R. L. Hall, 131-142. New York: Pergamon Press.

Walton, Hanes. 1972. Black Political Parties: An Historical and Political Analysis. NewYork: Free Press.

Walton, Hanes, and William H. Boone. 1974. "Black Political Parties: A Demographic Analysis." Journal of Black Studies 5: 86-96.

Walton, Hanes. 1985. Invisible Politics: Black Political Behavior. Albany: State University of New York Press.

Wellman, David T. 1977. Portraits of White Racism. New York: Cambridge University Press.

Welsing, Frances Cress. 1991. The Isis Papers: The Keys to the Colors. Chicago: Third World Press.

West, Cornel. 1993. Race Matters. New York: Vintage Books.

Wilson, E. O. 1978. On Human Nature. Cambridge, MA: Harvard University Press.

Wilson, William J. 1978. The Declining Significance of Race. Chicago: University of Chicago Press.

------. 1987. The Truly Disadvantaged. Chicago: University of Chicago Press.

Wolfman, Brunetta R. 1977. "The Communist Party, Always Out of Step." In Black Separatism and Social Reality: Rhetoric and Reason. Ed. R. L. Hall, 109-114. New York: Pergamon Press.

Wolpe, Harold. 1986. "Class Concepts, Class Struggle and Racism." In Theories of Race and Ethnic Relations, eds. J. Rex and D. Mason. Cambridge: Cambridge University Press.

Woodson, Carter G. [1933] 1990. The Mis-Education of the Negro. Trenton, NJ: AfricaWorld Press.

Wright, Bruce. 1993. Black Robes, White Justice. New York: Lyle Stuart.

Wright, Richard. [1957] 1964. White man, Listen! Garden City, NY: Anchor.

Yearwood, Lenox, S., ed. 1980. Black Organizations: Issues on Survival Techniques. Washington, DC: University Press of America.

Yette, Samuel F. 1975. The Choice: The Issue of Black Survival in America. New York: Berkley Medallion Books.